THE WHITE STAR

An Illustrated History 1870-1934

Paul Louden-Brown

SHIP PICTORIAL PUBLICATIONS
1991

Dedicated to my wife Elizabeth-Anne.

First Published in 1991 by Ship Pictorial Publications
3 College Close, Coltishall, Norfolk NR12 7DT.

© Copyright Paul Louden-Brown 1991

British Library Cataloguing in Publication Data
Louden-Brown, Paul
  The White Star line : an illustrated history 1870-1934.
  I. Title
  387.506541

ISBN 0 9516038 2 5

Ship Pictorial Series

S.P.P. 1   The Cunard Line (Peter W. Woolley & Terry Moore)
S.P.P. 2   The Union-Castle Line (Alan S. Mallett)
S.P.P. 3   The White Star Line (Paul Louden-Brown)
S.P.P. 4   Shaw Savill & Albion (Richard de Kerbrech)

Typeset, printed and bound by
Manchester Free Press, Paragon Mill, Jersey Street, Manchester M4 6FP.

CONTENTS

Cover illustration: OCEANIC II leaving New York

Back cover illustration: Hand-painted enamel ship's badge — R.M.S. CEDRIC

White Star Line motto — Praesto Persisto (Ready and Steadfast)

THOMAS HENRY ISMAY (1837-1899)
FOUNDER OF THE WHITE STAR LINE

FOREWORD

by

Michael Bower Manser

Great Grandson of Thomas Henry Ismay

The White Star Line's OCEANIC made her maiden voyage at the time the line's founder was gravely ill. Her passengers passed a resolution which conveyed their appreciation of the 'splendid vessel', expressed sympathy with T.H. Ismay in his 'trying illness' and ended 'we recognise in Mr. Ismay not only the sagacious man of business who has been foremost in all advances toward the present degree of perfection in ocean travel, but also a man of large benevolent feeling, who knows how to live for the service of others.'
This was written in 1899. The following half century was not without change and turbulence in the history of the White Star Line, and yet in the 1950's the GEORGIC and the BRITANNIC retained still, something of the quality and standard that had distinguished and differentiated the White Star Line from its competition in the latter decades of the nineteenth century.

The White Star Line inspired exceptional loyalty in its employees and its passengers. As a great grandson of the line's founder I may lack objectivity, but it can be persuasively argued, I think, that Thomas Henry Ismay set a lasting standard for his line which marked it in much the same way as its five pointed star and black topped buff funnels marked it. A writer on nineteenth century shipowners has compared him to a grass staircase with banisters of clipped yew, he had seen. 'I cannot help thinking' he says, 'that this staircase ascending upward, straight, regular, well ordered, firm in its setting, perfect in its surroundings, bears a strong resemblance to the life of Thomas Ismay.'

The history of the White Star Line is the history of an extraordinary enterprise initiated by someone whom the Times of 1899 described as a genius. There are moments of elation, tragedy and high drama. This book is a very welcome addition to the literature on merchant shipping in general and on one great shipping line in particular.

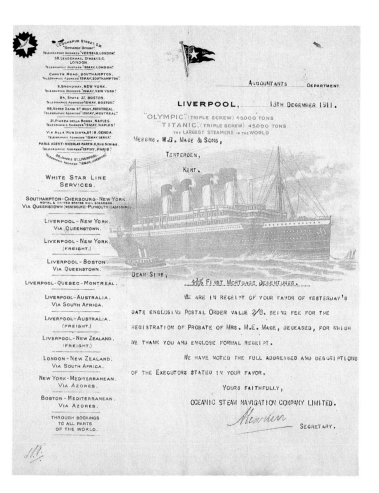

**WHITE STAR LINE
LETTERHEAD
ADVERTISING THE
NEW OLYMPIC & TITANIC**

INTRODUCTION

The White Star Line once a household name today is best remembered as the owner of the ill-fated TITANIC, lost on her maiden voyage after collision with an iceberg. The disaster marked a turning point in the company's fortunes. In financial difficulties after the American International Mercantile Marine Company (IMMCO) bought out White Star in 1902, the First World War and an urgent need for shipping, only temporarily revived the company's ailing finances.

By the end of the war a worldwide glut of tonnage together with reduced immigration to America, signalled a new period of financial struggle brought about largely by the enormous dividends taken up by IMMCO. During a meeting in the mid-twenties over the company's finances between the Chairman of White Star, Harold Sanderson and the President of IMMCO, P.A.S. Franklin, a senior manager recalled a heated discussion when Sanderson turned to Franklin and said 'you are not satisfied with robbing the White Star nest of all its eggs, but you look for them even before they are laid.'

It was not always like this. The company founded by Thomas Henry Ismay in 1869 was an immediate success, its ships the largest, finest and most profitable in service, even during the company's ownership by IMMCO, standards of quality and service remained but the magic of the Victorian days was long gone. White Star's purchase in 1927 by the Royal Mail Group did little to improve matters. Grandiose plans for a new 1,000 ft. — 60,000-ton motor liner came to nothing and this together with the share purchase of other lines put even more pressure on the hard pressed White Star Line. The crunch finally came in 1934, White Star was forced by the British Government to amalgamate with Cunard. Never again would the White Star burgee proudly fly over the finest fleet on the North Atlantic.

This book gathers together for the first time the most representative collection of rare illustrations of this famous company's ships.

Paul Louden-Brown
Miller's Cottage,
Canterbury.
November 1990.

A SHORT HISTORY OF THE WHITE STAR LINE

PART ONE

The White Star Line with its distinctive house flag, a red burgee with a five pointed white star, became one of the most famous and prestigious shipping lines of the nineteenth and twentieth centuries. So popular was the image and style of this great shipping line that its official title the Oceanic Steam Navigation Company is forgotten today and it is now remembered as the White Star Line. One of the company's founders who had the greatest influence on its development and on shipping in general, was Thomas Henry Ismay a man of vision and organisational genius, named in his lifetime the Mercantile Prince.

In 1868, Thomas Henry Ismay of Maryport, aged thirty, was already a director of the National Steam Navigation Company and concurrently running his own small fleet of sailing ships, trading as T.H. Ismay & Company. On 18 January that year he bought for £1,000 the goodwill and house flag, a red burgee with a five pointed white star, of a bankrupt company the White Star Line of British & Australian Ex-Royal Mail Packets. This company had been founded twenty three years earlier by two Liverpool businessmen, Henry Threlfell Wilson and John Pilkington. The opening of the Australian gold fields in 1851 brought prosperity to their company. They owned some of the most famous clipper ships of those days, including WHITE STAR, RED JACKET, CHARIOT OF FAME and SHALIMAR and by 1863 they had their first steamship ROYAL STANDARD. However, four years later following unwise business speculation by Wilson, the company was in serious financial difficulties. Unable to meet its debt of £527,000 owed to the Royal Bank of Liverpool, the company went into liquidation in 1867.

Ismay now revived the defunct service to Australia and New Zealand sailing his own ships on these routes. Looking for opportunities to expand he formed an association with Gustav Christian Schwabe, a prominent Liverpool businessman. Schwabe's nephew, Gustav Wilhelm Wolff had recently entered into partnership with Edward Harland in a shipbuilding business in Belfast. Schwabe was a major shareholder in the company and the BROUGHTON, named after his West Derbyshire house, had been built by Harland & Wolff in Belfast. Ismay agreed to buy the BROUGHTON on the understanding that through Harland & Wolff, Schwabe would provide a quarter of the capital with Edward Harland holding a stake in the vessel. By this time Harland & Wolff had built several iron steamships of a new and innovative design for the Bibby line's Mediterranean service. Schwabe, keen to invest more capital in shipping and as no further shares were available in Harland & Wolff, decided to strengthen his association with Ismay. In 1869, one year later, Schwabe invited Ismay to dine with him at Broughton Hall. Over an after dinner game of billiards he put the following proposition to Ismay; Harland & Wolff would build the ships for a new steamship company with full financial backing from Schwabe, who would more importantly secure further backing by other Liverpool businessmen. Ismay's acceptance of the proposal set the White Star Line on its long voyage of success and in to the annals of shipping history.

On 6 September the Oceanic Steam Navigation Company (OSNC) No. 4540, the official name of the White Star Line, was founded with a capital of £400,000 made up of four hundred £1,000 shares. Thomas H. Ismay had started his business only twelve years earlier with £2,000. Now at the age of thirty two he was able to buy £50,000 worth of shares, an enormous sum of money in those days, early proof of his business genius. Gustav C. Schwabe was amongst the new company's shareholders with 12 shares, becoming the chairman of OSNC until his retirement in 1876. Edward Harland and his partner Gustav Wilhelm Wolff also held shares. Other shareholders were George Hamilton Fletcher with 50 shares. James and John Dugdale with 12 each, and James Hainsworth with 10. The shipowner James K. Bibby also had large shareholdings. William Imrie, a friend and fellow apprentice of Ismay's younger days with Imrie, Tomlinson & Company joined him in 1870 and became a partner of the managing agents, renamed Ismay, Imrie & Company.

Schwabe had kept his word and now Ismay was in a position to honour his part of their agreement. The new company immediately commissioned Harland & Wolff to design and build four steamships. The company's relationship to its shipbuilder was unique. Contracts were never entered into, Harland & Wolff were simply instructed to design and build the finest vessels they could, adding their own profit margin to the total cost. Called 'cost plus' this method of charging its client for new shipbuilding and repairs lasted for over sixty years. In fact from 1869 untill 1919 there was never a single day in which Harland & Wolff had not a ship under construction for White Star. Edward Harland's designs for a new class of vessel built on the 10:1 scale created ships of classical symmetry and elegance with the graceful lines of a yacht. The first of these beautiful ships to be launched was OCEANIC I followed by the ATLANTIC, BALTIC I and REPUBLIC I. Harland's design had placed her saloon accommodation amid-ships rather than in the usual position over the stern, thereby avoiding the uncomfortable vibrations from the ships screws. The shipping fraternity expected Ismay to enter his new steamers into the Australian trade and therefore greeted with surprise the press announcements that the intended port of call was to be New York. The North Atlantic trade was congested and fiercely competitive, nevertheless, Ismay and his colleagues were convinced that they could profit from this trade, and so on 2 March 1871 the OCEANIC left Liverpool on her maiden voyage.

Profits from the North Atlantic trade were disappointingly low and in order to offset these poor returns, a service to India, through the Suez Canal (opened two years earlier in 1869) was introduced. By 1872 the company expanded its trade to include South America. After only one year it suffered a major blow when the ATLANTIC ran aground during a gale off Halifax with the loss of 588 lives. The South American trade route was cancelled and replaced a year later in 1875 by a Pacific service with liners on charter to the Occidental & Oriental Steam Navigation Company. Livestock was a regular and profitable cargo on some of White Star's ships but in 1898 the company made the decision to cease carrying livestock on their passenger liners. Following this policy CYMRIC had her intended space for cattle converted into steerage accommodation and cargo space.

Rival shipping companies regularly engaged in breaking each others Atlantic speed records and in 1872 the ADRIATIC I broke the record held by Cunard's SCOTIA. Over the next twenty years the speed record changed hands many times. In the early years the record had been held by the BALTIC I, GERMANIC and BRITANNIC I, and finally in 1891 by the TEUTONIC with an average speed of 20.35 knots. The White Star Line held the blue ribbon of the Atlantic, the Pacific, and the New Zealand trades. However, speed records were no longer an important company issue and the policy changed to give priority to the comfort of passengers and to offer a punctual and reliable service. This strategy placed White Star ahead of its competitors and brought considerable prosperity to the company and its shareholders. The liners were renowned for their luxurious accommodation and were called floating palaces, a fitting title, for they sailed with the crowned heads of Europe, the nobility, and the rich and famous onboard. In 1899, the company launched its finest and largest vessel OCEANIC II, the first ship to exceed the length of the GREAT EASTERN built over forty years earlier but as yet not her tonnage.

Sadly in November of that year, Thomas H. Ismay the shipping genius, respected and liked by all who served under him, died after a series of heart attacks at his home Dawpool House, Thurstaston, Cheshire at the age of 62 and was buried in the Parish churchyard. The great line he had founded continued into the twentieth century with his eldest son J. Bruce Ismay in control.

PART TWO

In 1900 the White Star Line was firmly established as one of the world's most profitable shipping lines. The company held the leading position in the North Atlantic passenger and freight carrying trade, and was actively engaged in the trans-Pacific trade with the Far East and the Mediterranean, with services from Great Britain to South Africa, Australia and New Zealand. From 1901 the company took delivery year by year of the CELTIC II, CEDRIC, BALTIC II and ADRIATIC II, some of the most profitable liners ever built for the North Atlantic trade, each in turn the largest ship in the World. Compared with Cunard, the White Star Line was in a strong position and had considered acquiring the Cunard Line but eventually decided to continue on its own. Thomas Ismay's saying, never let a weak man out of your trade, and so make room for a strong one, seems to have been followed wisely by the company.

The share capital of OSNC increased twice in 1872 first by 100 shares bringing it up to 500 then finally to 750 shares of £1,000 each. The company limited its shareholders dividends to 10-15% each year and surplus funds over £7,000,000 were invested in new ships. In this way the fleet of steamships was built up from one vessel of 3,808 tons in 1871 to a vast fleet of 213,297 tons by 1901. After lengthy negotiations, ownership of the Oceanic Steam Navigation Company passed into the hands of J. Pierpont Morgan an American banker and industrialist who had formed the International Mercantile Marine Company of New Jersey (IMMCO) with a share capital of $120,000,000. Each of Oceanic's shareholders received £13,750 per £1,000 share, a total of over £10,000,000. Along with the White Star Line the American, Atlantic Transport, Dominion, Leyland and Red Star lines made up the rest of the new IMMCO fleet. The

White Star ships were not put under the American flag, but remained under British registry by a clause in IMMCO's altered charter. Right from the start IMMCO was in difficulties, J. Bruce Ismay was offered and accepted the presidency becoming the combine's second president in 1903, a position he was to hold for ten years, after Clement A. Griscom of the Red Star Line resigned due to managerial difficulties, announced in the press as ill health.

White Star's reputation for good service and reliability enabled the company to become the group's major carrier on the North Atlantic run; the other members of the group transferred their finest ships and relinquished some of the more profitable routes so that this policy could be implemented. In 1907 the express route to New York was transferred from Liverpool to Southampton with four ships maintaining the service, TEUTONIC, MAJESTIC I, OCEANIC II and ADRIATIC II (at that time the largest liner in the World), calling at Cherbourg and Queenstown westbound and Plymouth and Cherbourg eastbound.

Growing competition from Cunard prompted White Star to replace the four ship service with three enormous ships, the largest to be built in the world. J. Bruce Ismay and Lord Pirrie head of Harland & Wolff met at Pirrie's London residence Downshire House to discuss and plan the new giant liners. The first of the new super class OLYMPIC was launched by Harland & Wolff, Belfast on the 20 October 1910 entering service on 14 June 1911 with, as one might expect, a great deal of publicity and celebrations. A year later on 10 April her sister TITANIC left the new White Star Dock, Southampton on her maiden voyage. She was the second of her class and therefore did not attract much publicity. However, six days later her name hit the headlines of the world's press and the lessons learnt from the disaster brought about tremendous changes in the regulations concerning the safety of life at sea.

With the advent of the First World War a large number of White Star vessels were taken over by the British Government as either armed merchant cruisers, troopships or hospital ships. Many famous ships were lost, OCEANIC II after she ran aground off Foula in the Shetland Isles in 1914; BRITANNIC II third sister of the Olympic Class, sunk by a mine or torpedo in the Mediterranean before she had even made a single commercial voyage; LAURENTIC I sunk by a German submarine while carrying £5,000,000 in gold bullion; ARABIC II, CYMRIC, AFRIC, CEVIC, DELPHIC and GEORGIC I all sunk by German U-Boats, a total of 148,145 tons. Altogether the company carried over half a million troops and 4,250,000 tons of cargo during the war years.

After the Armistice White Star's surviving ships were refitted prior to resuming peacetime service. The Liverpool-New York service resumed with the Big Four CELTIC II, CEDRIC, BALTIC II and ADRIATIC II all of which survived the war without serious damage. The New York-Mediterranean service resumed in July 1919 and the Southampton-New York run two months later with ADRIATIC II and LAPLAND transferred from the Red Star Line, which was later replaced by the OLYMPIC. To replace tonnage lost during the war German vessels were taken over as reparations. The first BERLIN was renamed ARABIC III after the loss of ARABIC II by torpedo attack. The COLUMBUS became HOMERIC and BISMARCK became MAJESTIC II, both running on the express service with

OLYMPIC. MAJESTIC II was the largest and fastest ship White Star ever owned. She was the larger sister of the United States Line LEVIATHAN, ex-VATERLAND and Cunard's BERENGARIA, ex-IMPERATOR.

The Dominion Line was taken over by the Leyland Line in 1921, consequently in 1925 the White Star-Dominion Joint Service which had been inaugurated in 1908, became simply White Star Line (Canadian Service). As a result of the resurgence of German shipping the Hamburg call started in 1922 was finished in 1926. Also in that year it was announced that the Royal Mail Steam Packet Company would purchase the entire share capital of Oceanic from IMMCO for £7,000,000. From 1 January 1927 the company once more became an entirely British concern. A strange part of the deal with IMMCO was that White Star's agency arrangements in the United States for bookings and ticket sales remained with IMMCO, a substantial loss of revenue for the Royal Mail Group.

Lord Pirrie's and White Star's dream was finally realised in 1928. The keel of a new 1,000 ft. — 60,000 ton superliner was laid down by Harland & Wolff, Belfast for the company's express service, she was to be called OCEANIC III and to be electrically propelled. The fluctuating financial climate in America made long term planning difficult and the American Government's restriction on the number of immigrants lead White Star to abandon the ambitious plans for OCEANIC III. Despite the American depression the company in 1930, with the help of Government loans, introduced BRITANNIC III, the first passenger motor vessel on the North Atlantic service. She was followed two years later by her sister GEORGIC II and together they signified a new approach to passenger travel, being the largest Cabin Class ships on the North Atlantic. They were more economical than steamships and more lucrative for the company than their existing conventional fleet of steamers. They also proved very popular with the growing number of tourist passengers cruising during the winter months from New York to the West Indies and the Mediterranean.

The early thirties was an unhappy time for shipping in general. The depression caused many ships to be laid up only to go eventually to the breaker's yard before their time. A former White Star manager for the United Stated commented; 'In my time in New York the White Star Line was the very top of the tree. It has suffered many vicissitudes since and is still suffering. I cannot imagine anything more unfortunate for that great and splendid company than to be swallowed up in one unmanageable concern under the aegis of the Royal Mail Company. The White Star Line has been sucked dry like the proverbial orange to pay dividends for the other concerns, while its opponents have been working up to its former proud position.'

Starved of funds for re-investment and showing losses for four years, White Star signed an agreement with Cunard on the 17 May 1934 to form a combined company to be known as Cunard-White Star Line Limited. The British Government had intervened in the discussions undertaking to finance the completion of the new 80,000 ton Cunarder No. 534, work on which had been suspended owing to the depression. White Star was very much the junior partner with ten ships of 285,680 tons to add to the combine, seven of which were scrapped by 1939. White Star's ships for the most part were technically superior and younger than Cunard's, but as the junior partner its fine fleet was sacrificed. After the Second World War only BRITANNIC III was left, LAURENTIC II was sunk in 1940 and GEORGIC II badly damaged in 1941, although she did re-enter service under British Government ownership and managed by Cunard. In 1947 the Cunard Steam Ship Company purchased the remaining 38% of White Star's stake in Cunard-White Star Limited and by 1949 they took overall control, Cunard-White Star became simply Cunard Line. GEORGIC II remained on charter to Cunard and retained her old White Star colours until she was scrapped in 1956. BRITANNIC III was the last of an illustrious line to carry the red burgee with a white five pointed star, continuing on the North Atlantic until she was scrapped in December 1960. With her passing one of the greatest shipping lines disappeared forever.

In the Merseyside Maritime Museum the main bell of BRITANNIC III is on display with the poignant inscription;

M.V. BRITANNIC
1930 — 1960

NOTES TO ILLUSTRATIONS

1. All illustrations are taken from the author's collection.
2. Roman numeral(s) following a ship's name indicate the first, second etc. vessel of that name in White Star Line service.
3. Dates following a ship's name indicate the length of time in White Star Line service.
4. Brief statistical details of each vessel illustrated are listed in the Index on pages 136-138.
5. Tonnage shown on some illustrations may differ from that shown in the Index. This is due to modifications during a ship's career.
6. The term 'class' indicates that the vessel in question is one of several ships of broadly similar design. The term 'sister ship(s)' indicates that these vessels were built to the same dimensions, specifications and power and were generally similar but not necessarily identical in appearance and layout.

ACKNOWLEDGEMENTS

I would like to take this opportunity to thank the following individuals and instituitions for their kind help and assistance;

J. Alderson Smith M.C., Simpson, North & Alderson Smith Solicitors & Notaries, Liverpool.
Kenneth Burnley, *The Wirral Journal*, Cheshire.
Michael Bustard, Tonbridge, Kent.
Canterbury City Library.
Robert Cleaver, Copy Print, Canterbury, Kent.
The Cork Examiner, Ireland.
Charles Hedgcock, Liverpool & London P & I Management Ltd., Liverpool.
Captain Peter H. King F.N.I., Hampshire.
Liverpool City Libraries.
Liverpool Maritime Museum.

Angela Louden-Brown, Tunbridge Wells, Kent.
Michael B. Manser, Northamptonshire.
Charles Nash, Cobh, Ireland.
National Maritime Museum, Greenwich, London.
Principle Registry of the Family Division, London.
Public Record Office, London.
Sea Breezes Magazine, Liverpool.
The University of Kent at Canterbury Library.
Peter W. Woolley, Bootle, Merseyside.
Mike Veissid, Shrewsbury, Shropshire.

WHITE STAR STEAMSHIPS

OCEANIC I (1871-1895)

OCEANIC pioneer steamship of the White Star Line built by Harland & Wolff, Belfast. 2 March 1871 maiden voyage on the Liverpool-New York service cancelled due to bearing problems. 28 March arrived at New York. Winter 1872 returned to builders for alterations including the installation of extra boilers and bunkering space. 1875 chartered to the Occidental & Oriental Steam Navigation Company for their new San Francisco-Yokohama-Hong Kong service. 22 August 1888 collided with the American steamer CITY of CHESTER in dense fog inside the Golden Gate, San Francisco, the latter sinking with the loss of 16 lives. 11 November 1889 arrived at San Francisco after record passage from Yokohama of 13 days, 14 hours and 6 minutes. Refit at Belfast abandoned after structural survey, sold for £8,000. February 1896 broken up on the Thames.

Sister ships: ATLANTIC, BALTIC I, REPUBLIC I, ADRIATIC I & CELTIC I

ATLANTIC (1871-1873)

Built by Harland & Wolff, Belfast in 1870 for the Liverpool-New York service. Engines by G. Forrester & Co., Liverpool. 20 March 1873 left Liverpool for New York under the command of Captain J. H. Williams. 31 March after fierce weather conditions only 127 tons of coal remained, course altered for Halifax. 1 April at 3.00 a.m. ATLANTIC ran onto the Marr's Rock, Meaghers Island near Halifax with the loss of 585 passengers and crew. At the subsequent inquiries in Canada and Britain, White Star were held to blame for sending the liner to sea short of coal, thus indirectly causing her loss. On appeal the Board of Trade ruled that fuel had nothing to do with her loss.

Sister ships: OCEANIC I, BALTIC I, REPUBLIC I, ADRIATIC I & CELTIC I

WHITE STAR LINE

ADRIATIC I (1872-1897)

Built by Harland & Wolff, Belfast in 1872. 11 March maiden voyage on the Liverpool-New York service arriving in 8 days, 14 hours, at an average speed of 16½ knots. October 1874 collided with Cunard's PARTHIA at New York ADRIATIC sustained slight damage to her port quarter. March 1875 ran down and sank the schooner COLUMBUS. December ran down and sank another sailing vessel believed to have been HARVEST QUEEN with the loss of all hands.

Sister ships: OCEANIC I, ATLANTIC, BALTIC I, REPUBLIC I & CELTIC I

R.M.S. "ADRIATIC"

AUGUST 4TH 1896

PEA SOUP
BEEF TEA

SARDINES
PICKLED OYSTERS
ROAST MUTTON, ONION SAUCE
ROAST BEEF
LAMB
CORNED OX TONGUE
BRAWN
SPICED BEEF
HAM
BOLOGNA SAUSAGE
CHICKEN

BAKED POTATOES

STEWED APPLES & RICE
SMALL PASTRY

CHEESE   SALAD

ADRIATIC
1ST. CLASS MENU

Bad luck seemed to follow ADRIATIC for on 19 July 1885 she ran down and sank the brigantine G.A. PIKE off the Tuskar Rock with the loss of five lives, ADRIATIC held to have been travelling at excessive speed. 1885 OSNC shareholders held presentation dinner on board in honour of T.H. Ismay and William Imrie managers of the White Star Line. 1888 Harland & Wolff fitted second class accommodation. 17 November 1897 last voyage on the Liverpool-New York service. 1898 laid up at Birkenhead, Liverpool. 12 February 1899 sold and broken up at Preston, Lancashire.

CELTIC I (1872-1891)
DECK PLAN

Built by Harland & Wolff, Belfast in 1872. Laid down as ARCTIC, renamed CELTIC, after the loss of the unlucky Collins liner of the same name. 17 October maiden voyage on the Liverpool-New York service. CELTIC was the second ship in the White Star fleet to be lit by gas, however this form of lighting was removed after a few voyages due to leaks caused by the ships movement. January 1874 towed by GAELIC into Queenstown after she lost her propeller blades. January 1883 she again suffered from a similar problem this time with a broken propeller shaft 24 hours out from New York, BRITANNIC towing her back to Liverpool. 19 May 1887 outward bound for Liverpool collided with BRITANNIC in dense fog. 1888 limited number of second class cabins fitted by Harland & Wolff. 1891 last voyage for White Star on return from New York laid up at Birkenhead, Liverpool. April 1893 sold to the Tingvalla Line, renamed AMERIKA sailing under the Danish flag. 1898 broken up at Brest.

Sister ships: OCEANIC I, ATLANTIC, BALTIC I, REPUBLIC I & ADRIATIC I

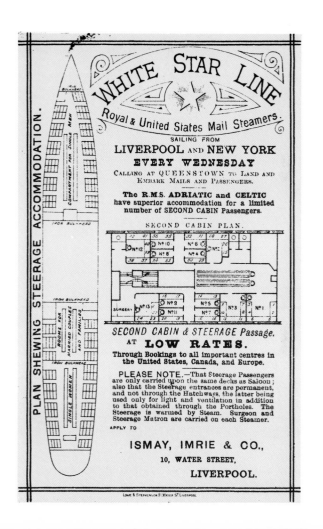

PLAN SHEWING STEERAGE ACCOMMODATION.

WHITE STAR LINE

Royal & United States Mail Steamers.

SAILING FROM

LIVERPOOL AND NEW YORK

EVERY WEDNESDAY

CALLING AT QUEENSTOWN TO LAND AND EMBARK MAILS AND PASSENGERS.

The R.M.S. ADRIATIC and CELTIC have superior accommodation for a limited number of SECOND CABIN Passengers.

SECOND CABIN PLAN.

SECOND CABIN & STEERAGE Passage.

AT **LOW RATES.**

Through Bookings to all important centres in the United States, Canada, and Europe.

PLEASE NOTE.—That Steerage Passengers are only carried upon the same decks as Saloon; also that the Steerage entrances are permanent, and not through the Hatchways, the latter being used only for light and ventilation in addition to that obtained through the Portholes. The Steerage is warmed by Steam, Surgeon and Steerage Matron are carried on each Steamer.

APPLY TO

ISMAY, IMRIE & CO.,

10, WATER STREET,

LIVERPOOL.

S.S. BRITANNIC

BRITANNIC I (1874-1902): & MAGNETIC IN THE MERSEY

Built by Harland & Wolff, Belfast in 1874. Originally laid down as HELLENIC. 25 June 1874 maiden voyage Liverpool-New York. Held both east and westbound speed records with passages of less than 7½ days. A novel design feature was an adjustable propeller shaft which allowed the propeller to run in smoother water, severe vibration however caused damage to bearings and the idea was dropped. 1881 collided and sank the Belfast steamer JULIA in the Irish Sea. July stranded in fog at Kilmore, refloated and beached for temporary repairs. Towed CELTIC to Liverpool with propeller problems, a flaw was discovered in BRITANNIC's own propeller shaft forcing the abandonment of her voyage. 1887 collided with CELTIC. 2 January 1890 collided with the brigantine CZAROWITZ in the Crosby Channel, Liverpool, cutting her in two. On her 318th. voyage later in the year BRITANNIC made her fastest passage in 7 days, 6 hours and 55 minutes at an average speed of 16.08 knots. October 1899 taken over as a Boer War troop transport. July 1903 sold to German shipbreakers for £11,500. 11 August towed to Hamburg for breaking up.

Sister ship: GERMANIC

GERMANIC (1875-1903)

Built by Harland & Wolff, Belfast in 1874. Designed by Sir Edward Harland, costing £200,000 to build. February 1876 won eastbound passage in 7 days, 15 hours and 17 minutes at an average speed of 15.70 knots. April 1877 won westbound passage in 7 days, 11 hours and 37 minutes. January had to put back to Waterford under sail after breaking her propeller shaft. 1895 triple expansion machinery fitted by Harland & Wolff increasing speed by one knot, passenger accommodation also modernised. Later in the year had the honour of being the first vessel to use the new floating landing stage at Liverpool. February 1899 sank during a blizzard at New York while coaling and taking on cargo. 23 February refloated and returned to Belfast under her own power for refitting. Photographed in the River Mersey.

Sister ship: BRITANNIC I

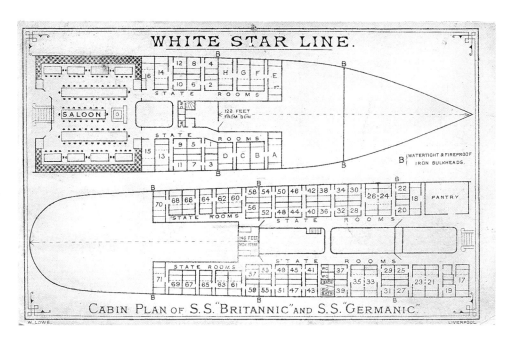

CABIN PLAN OF S.S. "BRITANNIC" AND S.S. "GERMANIC."

GERMANIC DECK PLAN

September 1903 last voyage for White Star after 28 years service. Transferred to the Dominion Line, renamed OTTAWA. 1910 sold to the Turkish Government for £20,000, renamed GUL DJEMAL. 1915 sunk by a British submarine while serving as a troop transport, later raised with the assistance of the German Navy. 1920 entered the emigrant trade from the Mediterranean and Black Sea ports to New York. 1923 stranded on rocks later refloated, requiring only minor repairs. Name revised to GULCEMAL (TURKIYE) under the ownership of Turkiye Seyrisefain Idaresi. 1933 after running ashore in the Sea of Marmora, transferred to coastal trading. 1949 storage ship at Istanbul, engines still intact but super structure cut down. 1950 converted in to a floating hotel. October towed to Messina, Sicily for breaking up after a remarkable career spanning 75 years.

TEUTONIC (1889-1914)

TEUTONIC was the first ship to be built with a subsidy from the British Admiralty so that in time of war or national emergency she could be converted quickly for naval operations. Designed by Alexander Carlisle as an Armed Merchant Cruiser she was the first vessel in the White Star fleet to be fitted with twin screws and not to carry sails. 19 January 1889 launched the first vessel fitted out at Harland & Wolff's new Alexandra Graving Dock. August attended the Spithead Naval Review as an Armed Merchant Cruiser inspected by Kaiser Wilhelm II and the Prince of Wales Photographed in the Solent.

Sister ship: MAJESTIC I

TEUTONIC OFFICERS & CREW AT SPITHEAD

26 June 1897 officers and crew pose for the official company photographer at the Spithead Naval Review. TEUTONIC took part in Queen Victoria's Diamond Jubilee celebrations with a review of the fleet, with 370 specially invited shareholders and guests onboard. The ship's armament of eight 4.7 inch quick fire, and eight Nordenfelt machine guns were fitted at Liverpool in just 24 hours, half the time laid down by the Admiralty. Thomas H. Ismay and his son J. Bruce Ismay were invited for a short trip in Charles Parson's TURBINA, at Spithead to prove to the Admiralty the high speeds turbine engines could achieve.

TEUTONIC 1ST. CLASS DINING SALON

TEUTONIC's magnificent dining saloon photographed on this early stereoscopic card published by Underwood & Underwood in the 1890's was sold as a souvenir to passengers onboard.

TEUTONIC 1ST. CLASS MAIN STAIRCASE

Harland & Wolff's master craftsmen surpassed themselves with TEUTONIC's main staircase carved from solid mahogany and descending through three decks.

S.S. "TEUTONIC" LEAVING PORTSMOUTH HARBOUR.

TEUTONIC LEAVING PORTSMOUTH HARBOUR

1900 taken over as a Boer War troop transport. 1907 transferred to the Southampton-New York service. 1911 transferred to the White Star-Dominion Line service to Canada. 12 September 1914 taken over as an Armed Merchant Cruiser. 16 August 1915 purchased by the Admiralty and fitted with 6 inch guns. December 1916 laid up. October 1917 recommissioned and rejoined the 10th. Cruiser Squadron. November transferred to the 2nd. Cruiser Squadron. 1918 transferred to the Shipping Controller for service as a troopship. 1920 put up for sale by the Ministry of Shipping, withdrawn and resumed trooping duties. 1921 laid up in Cowes Roads. July sold to Dutch shipbreakers, towed to Rotterdam. September resold to German shipbreakers and broken up at Emden.

WHITE STAR LINE.

R.M.S. "MAJESTIC"
565 FEET LONG, 10,146 TONS,
18,000 HORSE POWER.

Services to New York, South Africa,
Australia, and New Zealand.
ISMAY, IMRIE & CO., LONDON & LIVERPOOL.

MAJESTIC I (1890-1914)

Built by Harland & Wolff, Belfast. 2 April 1890 maiden voyage on the Liverpool-New York service. July 1891 won westbound speed record Queenstown-Sandy Hook in 5 days, 18 hours and 8 minutes at an average speed of 20.1 knots. 13 December 1899 began service as a Boer War troop transport. 1902-03 returned to builders for refitting, masts reduced to two, funnels heightened and extra boilers fitted increasing her tonnage to 10,147 GRT. 1907 transferred to the Southampton-New York service.

Sister ship: TEUTONIC

WHITE STAR LINE.

R.M.S. "MAJESTIC"

MAJESTIC AT COWES

November 1911 laid up at Bidston Dock, Birkenhead as a reserve ship. May 1912 replaced TITANIC on the Southampton-New York service. 14 January 1914 last sailing to New York on return sold for £25,000. 5 May arrived at Thomas W. Ward, Morecambe for breaking up. August demolition of MAJESTIC had progressed so far that it was impossible to retrieve her for war service.

NOMADIC I (1891-1903)

Built by Harland & Wolff, Belfast in 1891 as a livestock carrier. 24 April maiden voyage on the Liverpool-New York service. 1893 after the tragic loss of her sister ship NARONIC, rumours were rife that she had turned turtle and sunk. White Star subjected NOMADIC, where she lay in the Alexandra Dock, Liverpool, to severe stability tests in order to prove her sea worthiness, passing all tests with flying colours. October 1899 first White Star liner requisitioned for Boer War service as H.M.T. No. 34 a horse transporter and storeship. 1903 sold to Dominion Line, initially retaining her original name. 1904 renamed CORNISHMAN. July 1921 transferred to Frederick Leyland & Company under the same name, this appears to have been a transfer on paper only as CORNISHMAN continued to run in her Dominion colours and on the same routes. March 1926 sold for £10,500. 12 March arrived at Thomas W. Ward's yards, Hayle, Cornwall for breaking up.

Sister ship: NARONIC

MAGNETIC (1891-1932)

Built by Harland & Wolff, Belfast in 1891. 6 June delivered to White Star, designed as a passenger tender and fresh water replenisher for use at Liverpool. Fitted out for tug duties, meeting sailing ships of the line 100 miles out and towing them into Liverpool. The practice was stopped, however, after MAGNETIC got into difficulties due to her top heavy design. Employed for occasional river and coastal cruises, T.H. Ismay often used her to take underprivileged children for pleasure trips. June 1897 escorted TEUTONIC as tender at the Diamond Jubilee Naval Review, Spithead. 3 October 1925 caught fire and beached at Tranmere, restored by Harland & Wolff, Belfast. December 1932 sold to Alexandra Towing Co., Liverpool, renamed RYDE for use at Southampton, plan cancelled. RYDE continued in service at Liverpool. 1934 stationed at Llandudno for coastal excursions towards Rhyl, making the trip up to three times a day. 1935 sold. 8 August left the Mersey for Port Glasgow and breaking up.

R.M.S. "GOTHIC."   The Library.

GOTHIC (1894-1906): FIRST CLASS LIBRARY

Built by Harland & Wolff, Belfast in 1893. Largest vessel to enter the port of London. 30 November maiden voyage to Wellington, New Zealand. Made several record passages to New Zealand. First return voyage arrived three days ahead of schedule. 1894 set record passage of 37 days, 10 hours and 16 minutes at an average speed of 14.16 knots for the whole 12,910 mile voyage. June 1906 on passage Wellington-London fire discovered in wool cargo a few miles out from Plymouth, the crew thought they had put the fire out however it broke out once again becoming so serious that the ship's seacocks had to be opened. Scuttled in the shallow waters of Plymouth's Cattewater, settling with a heavy list. Later raised making the Port of London under her own power. Returned to Harland & Wolff for refitting, her elegant first class accommodation removed and replaced by emigrant accommodation.

"Gothland".

GOTHLAND ON THE GUNNER ROCKS

1907 Gothic transferred to Red Star, renamed GOTHLAND sailing under the Belgian flag. 23 June 1914 ran aground on the Gunner Rocks, off the Scilly Isles while homeward bound from Canada. Remained aground for three days, towed off after her 281 passengers had been taken off. Extensive repairs at Southampton lasted many months. March 1925 final voyage for Red Star. January 1926 sold for £16,000 broken up at Bo'ness, Firth of Forth.

CEVIC (1894-1914)

Built by Harland & Wolff, Belfast in 1893. 12 January 1894 maiden voyage on the Liverpool-New York service she was a livestock carrier. 1908 with the depression closing the New York cargo service she transferred to the Australian service. 1910 made an experimental voyage to Australia via the Suez Canal, her extra draught caused her to ground so she was placed back on her normal route via the Cape. December 1914 sold to the British Admiralty and converted into a dummy of H.M.S. Queen Elizabeth. 1916 converted into an oil tanker, renamed BAYOL. 1917 transferred to the Shipping Controller, renamed BAYLEAF under Lane & McAndrews management. 1920 sold to Anglo Saxon Petroleum Co. (Shell), renamed PYRULA. 25 July 1933 sold to Henrico Haupt for breaking up at Genoa.

WHITE STAR LINE

"CYMRIC" AT BOSTON.

CYMRIC (1898-1916)

Built by Harland & Wolff, Belfast in 1898. 5 February delivered to Liverpool, the largest cargo ship in the world, with accommodation for 258 1st. and 1,160 3rd. class passengers. CYMRIC was designed as an enlarged version of GEORGIC I. Transporting cattle on the same ship as passengers was proving very unpopular so her projected cattle space was converted for steerage passengers and cargo. 11 February maiden voyage on the Liverpool-New York service. 1 January 1900 served as a Boer War troop transport No. 74 for two return voyages to the Cape. 8 May 1916 torpedoed and sunk by U-20 140 miles W.N.W. off the Fastnet Rock, foundered the following day with the loss of five crewmen.

WHITE STAR LINE

"AFRIC" APPROACHING MELBOURNE

AFRIC (1899-1917)

Built by Harland & Wolff, Belfast for White Star's new Colonial Service to Australia. Designed to carry freight and livestock with accommodation for 320 cabin class passengers only. Along with her sisters these fine vessels set a new standard of comfort and size on this route. 8 February maiden voyage Liverpool-New York, returned to Harland & Wolff for minor improvements increasing tonnage to 11,948 GRT. 9 September finally made her first voyage on intended route to Sydney, Australia via the Cape. 1915 requisitioned by the Australian Government as a troop transport. February 1917 torpedoed enroute from Liverpool to Plymouth by UC-66 12 nautical miles S.S.W. of Eddystone Lighthouse. Captain Thompson commander of AFRIC received orders not to pass the Eddystone without first contacting one of the patrol boats in the area. 1 February arrived off the Eddystone at seven o'clock and spent ten hours looking for her escorts. It is hardly surprising that she was torpedoed in broad daylight the following morning.

Sister Ships: MEDIC, PERSIC, RUNIC II & SUEVIC

MEDIC (1899-1928)

Built by Harland & Wolff, Belfast in 1899. 3 August 1899 maiden voyage Liverpool-Australia. Return voyage carried Australian troop reinforcements and horses to South Africa for the Boer War campaign. September arrived at Albany the largest vessel to enter the port and the largest on the South African and Australian service. First World War served as a troop transport at Suvla Bay during the Gallipoli campaign. December 1927 last voyage for White Star on the Liverpool-Sydney service on return laid up and offered for sale. June 1928 sold to a Dutch whaling company, converted on the Mersey by the Birkenhead firm of H.C. Grayson into a bulk whale oil factory mother ship. Renamed HEKTORIA, working with the whaling fleets off South Georgia. 11 September 1942 torpedoed and sunk by U-608 in the North Atlantic whilst in service as a British Ministry of War Transport oil tanker.

Sister ships: AFRIC, PERSIC, RUNIC II & SUEVIC

Alexandra Graving Dock, Belfast, with great Atlantic Liners.

OCEANIC II (1899-1914): FITTING OUT ALONGSIDE THE ALEXANDRA GRAVING DOCK

Built by Harland & Wolff, Belfast. Launched on Saturday 14 January 1899. OCEANIC was the largest liner in the world until 1901. Built at a cost of £750,000 she was the first vessel to exceed the length of the GREAT EASTERN but not as yet her tonnage.

Sister ship: OLYMPIC I (Projected but cancelled after the death of T.H Ismay).

7254 A

R.M.S. OCEANIC (WHITE STAR LINE)
17,274 TONS. LENGTH, 704 FT. BREADTH, 68 FT.

ROTARY PHOTO. E.C.

OCEANIC IN THE MERSEY

6 September maiden voyage on the Liverpool-New York service under the command of Captain John G. Cameron R.N.R., making the passage in 6 days, 2 hours and 27 minutes at an average speed of 19.57 knots. 1905 mutiny onboard, 33 firemen were later jailed.

R.M.S. "OCEANIC"

Hors d'œuvres

Spider's Kidneys   Flea's Eyes
Humming Bird's Tongues

—

Purée of Blubber   Cod Liver Oil Broth

—

Shark's Fins à la Maître d'Hôtel
Broiled Octopus

—

Vol-au-Vent of Worms
Curried Cockroaches

—

Devilled Albatross   Fricassi of Buzzard

Camel's Humps

Hyæna à la Forêt

—

Angel's Eyes   Mermaid's Mers
Mammas' Black Looks
Pretty Girl's Kisses   Glad Eyes

—

Caviare en Confiture

—

Candied Anchovies   Peppermints in Paraffin
Vaseline in Grape Fruit
Toad's Necks in Syrup

OCEANIC, 1ST. CLASS MENU

'April Fools' Day' menu for first class passengers. OCEANIC's dining saloon was certainly no joke. The Marine Engineer described it as follows; 'The room is remarkable for its decoration. It is panelled in oak washed with gold, while its saloon dome (designed by a Royal Academician), decorated with allegorical figures, representing Great Britain and the United States and Liverpool and New York, is very beautiful and striking.'

OCEANIC STERN-MOUNTED 4.7 INCH GUN

22 May 1907 last sailing on the Liverpool-New York service, transferred to the new Southampton-New York express service. 8 August 1914 on the outbreak of hostilities commissioned as H.M.S. OCEANIC, an Armed Merchant Cruiser serving with the 10th Cruiser Squadron.

OCEANIC ON THE ROCKS

27 August sailed from Southampton on patrol to the Northern Approaches under the command of a Royal Naval officer Captain W.F. Slayter. OCEANIC's regular commander Captain H. Smith R.N.R. was kept on in an advisory capacity. 8 September ran aground in a flat calm and good weather on the Hoevdi Rocks, 2 miles east of Foula Island in the Shetland Isles. Confusion over her position, compounded by the two commanders overruling each others orders led to the accident. 11 September all attempts to save the ship failed, declared a total constructive loss. 29 September after a gale the wreck disappeared completely from view.

S.S. PERSIC 12000 TONS

PERSIC (1899-1927): AT LIVERPOOL LANDING STAGE

Built by Harland & Wolff, Belfast in 1899. 16 November delivered to White Star. 7 December maiden voyage on the Liverpool-Australia via Capetown service. Return voyage carried troops and horses for the Boer War campaign. October 1900 rescued crew of the sailing schooner MADURA, which was drifting on fire in mid- Atlantic. Requisitioned during the War by the British Government. September 1918 torpedoed by a German U-Boat in the Mediterranean off Sicily, managed to reach port for repairs. July 1919 released from Government service and returned to the Australian run. July 1927 sold for £25,000, broken up in Holland.

Sister ships: AFRIC, MEDIC, RUNIC II & SUEVIC

RUNIC II (1900-1929): PASSENGERS CRICKET MATCH

Built by Harland & Wolff, Belfast in 1900. 19 January 1901 maiden voyage to Australia. November towed disabled Union Castle liner DUNOTTAR CASTLE I into Dakar. This unusual postcard photograph and published onboard was posted on arrival in Australia in March 1910 with the following message; 'Cricket match on S/S Runic Ladies v Gentlemen, Ladies won easily. I have marked Elsie & Winnie with X. We are all very well and healthy, we have a fine boat & very nice lot of passengers, plenty of games, good food & cheap tobacco...' what more could one ask for! 1917 requisitioned for war service. April 1919 released back to commercial service. October 1921 returned to Harland & Wolff for reconditioning and reconstruction of passenger accommodation. 1928 collided with H.M.S. LONDON, off Gourock pier, on the Clyde, RUNIC suffering stern damage. 1929 sold to the Sevilla Whaling Company, converted in to a whale factory ship, renamed NEW SEVILLA. October 1940 torpedoed and sunk by U-138 off Galway, Ireland with the loss of two lives.

30   Sister ships: AFRIC, MEDIC, PERSIC & SUEVIC

SUEVIC (1901-1928): OFF GRAVESEND

Built by Harland & Wolff, Belfast in 1900. 23 March 1901 maiden voyage on the Liverpool-Australia via Capetown service. Return voyage carried Australian troops for the Boer War campaign.

Sister ships: AFRIC, MEDIC, PERSIC & RUNIC II

WRECK OF THE WHITE STAR LINER "SUEVIC" AT THE LIZARD CORNWALL, MARCH 17TH 1907. No 7.

SUEVIC ON THE ROCKS

Sunday 17 March 1907 while steaming home to Liverpool via Plymouth at 13 knots, SUEVIC ran aground in fog and drizzle on the Stag Rock, part of the Manacles near the Lizard. Her 382 passengers were safely taken ashore in the ships own lifeboats with the help of the local R.N.L.I. lifeboats. Most of her cargo valued at £400,000 including a large consignment of frozen lamb carcasses was saved.

SALVAGE OPERATIONS ON THE WHITE STAR LINER "SUEVIC". THE X X INDICATES WHERE SHE IS BEING CUT IN TWO. THE A.A PORTION WILL BE LEFT ON THE ROCKS.

CUTTING SUEVIC'S HULL APART

27 March weather worsened, and SUEVIC went further onto the rocks. RANGER of the Liverpool & Glasgow Salvage Association was now standing by. With her stern section still intact and undamaged the decision was taken to save her by cutting the liner in two just aft of the bridge. As this was before the use of oxy-acetylene cutting equipment, explosives had to be placed in a non-stop twenty-four hour operation around the ships hull by divers and engineers. On the high tide on Tuesday 2 April at 7.00 a.m., with SUEVIC's own engines going full astern and the tugs RANGER, HERCLANEUM and BLAZER straining on steel hawsers attached to her stern the final explosives were detonated and she finally parted from her bow.

WRECK OF THE "SUEVIC" SHOWING THE BOW PORTION (ABOUT 184 FT) WHICH IS LEFT ON THE ROCKS AT THE LIZARD.

REMAINING BOW SECTION ON THE ROCKS

Waves begin the demolition of SUEVIC's bow which soon disappeared from view.

S.S. SUEVIC IN SOUTHAMPTON DOCKS 'PRIL 4 1907

SALVAGED STERN SECTION IN DRYDOCK

4 April stern section arrived at Southampton's Test Quay. Two days later moved into No. 6 Graving Dock where the water was pumped out and a full inspection of SUEVIC could take place. There was remarkably little damage to the stern section, only three starboard plates near the keel were slightly dented.

After the Launch of Bow of S.S. Suevie from Queen's Island, Belfast, 5th Oct., 1907.

NEW BOW SECTION AFTER LAUNCH

5 October the new 212 ft. long bow section was launched bow first. 19 October towed to Southampton by the tugs PATHFINDER and BLAZER.

WILLSTEED   S S SUEVIC'S NEW BOW AT SOUTHAMPTON. 26TH OCT 1907.   I.

NEW BOW SECTION AT SOUTHAMPTON

26 October new bow arrived and was moved into No. 6 Graving Dock. 4 November joining up operations begin, lasting two months. SUEVIC was out of service for eighteen months, White Star, however were so confident in Harland & Wolff and John I. Thorneycroft (in charge of the rebuilding operation) that they readvertised her new sailings even before the new bow was completed at Belfast. 14 January 1908 re-entered the Australian service. 1917 requisitioned by the British Government. 20 February 1919 returned to commercial service after refitting at Belfast, passenger accommodation reduced to 266 second class. October 1928 sold for £35,000 to Yngar Hvistendahl Finnvhal, Tonsburg for conversion to a whale oil factory ship, renamed SKYTTEREN. Interned at Gothenburg on the outbreak of hostilities. 1 April 1942 crew attempted to escape to Britain, the German Navy intercepted SKYTTEREN, her crew scuttled the vessel off the coast of Sweden before she could be boarded.

A Modern Liner.   *Ready for Launching.*

CELTIC II (1901-1928): **ON THE STOCKS**

Built by Harland & Wolff, Belfast in 1901. The first of the Big Four and the last vessel ordered by Thomas H. Ismay before his death. Completed as the largest liner in the world her design proved so successful that White Star quickly ordered three more. 26 July 1901 maiden voyage on the Liverpool-New York service. 20 October 1914 commissioned as an Armed Merchant Cruiser, fitted with eight 6 inch guns. 1919 reconditioned by Harland & Wolff, Belfast. January 1920 resumed commercial service.

Sister ships: **CEDRIC, BALTIC II & ADRIATIC II**

CELTIC AGROUND AT COBH

10 December 1928 entering Cobh (Queenstown) harbour during a storm CELTIC went aground on the Calf Rocks adjacent to the harbour entrance. Despite several attempts to salvage her, she remained ashore and became a total constructive loss. Wreck sold to Peterson & Albeck, Copenhagen demolition completed in 1933.

ATHENIC (1902-1927): AS A TROOP TRANSPORT

Built by Harland & Wolff, Belfast in 1901. First of three ATHENIC class liners built for the White Star-Shaw Savill & Albion Joint Service to Australia and New Zealand. 14 February 1902 maiden voyage on the London-Wellington, New Zealand service.

Sister ships: CORINTHIC & IONIC II

ATHENIC AT LYTTLELTON

August 1914 requisitioned as a New Zealand troop transport. October 1927 last commercial voyage for White Star. May 1928 sold to the British & Norwegian Whaling Company for £33,000, renamed PELAGOS. January 1941 captured by the German Auxiliary Cruiser PINGUIN, taken to Bordeaux with a prize crew. Sunk during naval experiments in 1944. After the War raised and placed back in service. 1962 sold for scrapping. June broken up at Hamburg.

S 634,3   SHAW SAVILL & ALBION CO'S S.S. "CORINTHIC"

CORINTHIC (1902-1931)

Built by Harland & Wolff, Belfast in 1902 for White Star's Australian service. 20 November 1902 maiden voyage to New Zealand. 1917-1919 operated under the British Government's Liner Requisition Scheme. March 1927 collided with H.M.S. QUEEN ELIZABETH while leaving Malta, destroying the battleships portside sternwalk. August 1931 sold to Hughes, Bolckow & Company for £10,250 and scrapped at Blyth. April 1932 demolition completed by Swan Hunter & Wigham Richardson at Wallsend.

Sister ships: ATHENIC & IONIC II

IONIC. W.S. LINE.

IONIC II (1902-1934)

Built by Harland & Wolff, Belfast in 1902 for White Star's Australian service. 16 January 1903 maiden voyage to New Zealand. 1917-1919 operated under the British Government's Liner Requisition Scheme. 1929 converted to cabin and third class liner. 1934 transferred to Shaw Savill & Albion after the amalgamation of Cunard and White Star. December 1936 sold to Japanese shipbreakers for £31,500 and broken up at Osaka.

Sister ships: ATHENIC & CORINTHIC

WHITE STAR LINE

"CEDRIC" LEAVING LIVERPOOL

CEDRIC (1903-1931)

Built by Harland & Wolff, Belfast in 1903 for White Star's Liverpool-New York service. 11 February 1903 maiden voyage to New York. November 1914 converted to an Armed Merchant Cruiser and served along with TEUTONIC in the 10th. Cruiser Squadron.

Sister ships: CELTIC II, BALTIC II & ADRIATIC II

CEDRIC AT LIVERPOOL LANDING STAGE

29 January 1918 rammed the Canadian Pacific liner MONTREAL sailing with convoy HG 47. MONTREAL was taken in tow but sank the next day 14 miles off the Mersey Bar Lightship. September 1919 refitted by Harland & Wolff, Belfast.

The Managers of the White Star Line
request the honour of the Company of

Mr C. Concanon

at an Inspection of the Twin-Screw Royal Mail Steamer
"CEDRIC" — 21,227 TONS
(AFTER CONVERSION TO A CABIN CARRIER)

at Huskisson Dock (West Side) Liverpool, at 12 noon,
on Friday, October 22nd 1926.
Luncheon on board at 1 p.m.
Rail order for travelling to Liverpool and return will be sent to you on receipt of your acceptance.

R.S.V.P. White Star Line,
(Publicity Department)
30, James Street, Liverpool.

A reply not later than Oct. 15th will be appreciated. Kindly mark envelope "Cedric Function."

CEDRIC INVITATION CARD

1926 converted to a Cabin Class liner, this is one of the invitation cards sent to guests. September 1931 sold to Thomas W. Ward Shipbreakers for £22,150. January 1932 broken up at Inverkeithing.

83   LANDING STAGE & S. S. "CANADA" LIVERPOOL.

CANADA (1903-1926)

Built by Harland & Wolff, Belfast in 1896 for the Dominion Line. 1902 transferred to White Star. 13 March 1903 first voyage on the new White Star-Dominion Line Joint Service to Canada. 1914 requisitioned as a troop transport, serving during the Dardanelles campaign. November 1918 released from Government service. Converted to a Cabin Class liner. August 1926 sold to Italian shipbreakers for £17,000, broken up at Genoa.

R.MS. "Victorian"

Length - - 520 ft.
Breadth - - 60,4 ,,
Depth - - 38.0 ,,

VICTORIAN (1903-1914)

Built by Harland & Wolff, Belfast in 1895 for the Leyland Line as VICTORIAN. 28 February 1903 transferred to White Star management. 24 April first voyage on the Liverpool-New York service. 1904 transferred again to the company's cargo service. 1914 renamed RUSSIAN. October 1916 attacked by German U-Boat. 14 December sunk by UB-43 210 miles of Malta with the loss of 28 lives.

ARABIC II (1903-1915)

Laid down by Harland & Wolff, Belfast in 1902 for Atlantic Transport as the MINNEWASKA. On takeover by IMMCO, transferred to White Star and modified to their own design. 18 December launched as ARABIC II. 26 June 1903 maiden voyage on the Liverpool-New York service.

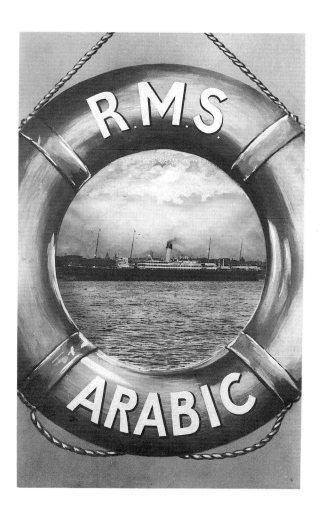

49

"GINGER"
"S. S. ARABIC"

GINGER, THE SHIP'S CAT

19 August 1915 torpedoed while enroute for New York with 200 passengers by U-24 off the Old Head of Kinsale, with the loss of 44 lives. ARABIC was White Star's first wartime loss. Sadly Ginger the ship's faithful cat was also lost.

WHITE STAR LINE.

R.M.S. "ROMANIC" at Palermo

ROMANIC (1903-1912)

Built by Harland & Wolff, Belfast in 1898 for Dominion Line as NEW ENGLAND. November 1903 transferred to White Star, renamed ROMANIC. 19 November first voyage on the Liverpool-Boston service. January 1912 sold to Allan Line, renamed SCANDINAVIAN. 9 July 1923 sold to F. Rijsdijk, Rotterdam for scrapping. 16 July re-sold to Klasmann & Lentze, Emden. October scrapped at Hamburg.

CRETIC (1903-1923)

Built by Hawthorn Leslie & Company, Hebburn, Newcastle in 1902 for the Leyland Line as HANOVERIAN. April 1903 transferred to Dominion Line, renamed MAYFLOWER. November transferred again this time to White Star, renamed CRETIC, remaining on the Liverpool- Boston service. June 1923 sold back to Leyland Line renamed DEVONIAN II, also for a time operated by Red Star without name change. January 1929 sold for breaking up to P. & W. MacLellan, Bo'ness, Firth of Forth.

WHITE STAR LINE

"REPUBLIC" AT NAPLES

REPUBLIC II (1903-1909)

Built by Harland & Wolff, Belfast in 1903 for Dominion Line as COLUMBUS. 1903 transferred to White Star, renamed REPUBLIC. 17 December first voyage on the Liverpool-Boston service. October 1904 transferred to the New York-Mediterranean service.

CRUMPLED BOWS OF FLORIDA AFTER COLLISION WITH REPUBLIC

23 January 1909 REPUBLIC with 525 passengers and 297 crew was rammed off Nantucket by the Lloyd Italiano liner FLORIDA. Passengers along with most of the crew were transferred to FLORIDA. The following day despite the efforts of her skeleton crew to save her, REPUBLIC sank. FLORIDA made it safely to New York with the escort of BALTIC II, called up by wireless, one of its earliest recorded uses.

WHITE STAR
LINE.

TWIN-SCREW S.S. "CANOPIC,"
12,268 TONS.

CANOPIC (1904-1925)

Built by Harland & Wolff, Belfast in 1900 for the Dominion Line as COMMONWEALTH. 1903 sold to White Star, renamed CANOPIC. 14 January first voyage on the Liverpool-Boston service. January 1904 transferred to the Liverpool-Mediterranean service. 26 April 1917 operated under the British Government's Liner Requisition Scheme. February 1919 returned to commercial service. October 1925 sold and broken up at Briton Ferry, South Wales.

CUFIC II (1904-1923): STEWARDS POSING ON THE BOAT DECK

Built by Harland & Wolff, Belfast in 1895 for West India & Pacific Steam Ship Co., as AMERICAN. 1898 chartered by Atlantic Transport. 1900 sold to Leyland Line. 1904 transferred to White Star for the Australian service. 21 May first voyage Liverpool-Sydney, Australia. 1917-1919 operated under the British Government's Liner Requisition Scheme. January 1924 sold for scrapping at Genoa. Reprieved and placed back in service renamed ANTARTICO. 1927 sold renamed MARIA GIULIA. November 1932 finally sold and broken up at Genoa.

BALTIC II (1904-1932)

Built by Harland & Wolff, Belfast in 1904. Third of White Star's Big Four, delivered as the largest vessel in the world after a 28 ft. mid-ships section was fitted during building increasing her tonnage by 2,840. 29 June maiden voyage on the Liverpool-New York service. During the first world war BALTIC carried over 32,000 U.S. and Canadian servicemen.

Sister ships: CELTIC II, CEDRIC & ADRIATIC II

57

WHITE STAR LINE. R.M.S. BALTIC, CEDRIC AND CELTIC
THIRD CLASS LOUNGE

R.M.S. BALTIC, CEDRIC & CELTIC: 3RD. CLASS LOUNGE

1927 BALTIC was the first of the Big Four to be converted to a cabin class liner with altered accommodation for 393 cabin, 339 tourist and 1,150 third class passengers. September 1932 last commercial voyage. January 1933 sold to Japanese shipbreakers.

GALLIC I (1907-1913)

Built by J. Scott & Co., Kinghorn, Fife in 1896 for Birkenhead Ferries Department as BIRKENHEAD III, with compound engines and paddles. March 1907 sold to White Star, renamed GALLIC for tender service at Cherbourg, after the introduction of the new Southampton-New York service. 1913 sold after the introduction of the tenders NOMADIC II and TRAFFIC II. Scrapped at Garston on the River Mersey.

ADRIATIC AT THE STAGE

ADRIATIC II (1907-1934)

Built by Harland & Wolff, Belfast, ordered December 1903, not delivered until May 1907. Last of the Big Four and the largest vessel in the world until the advent of Cunard's MAURETANIA. 8 May maiden voyage on the Liverpool-New York service. Placed on White Star's new Southampton-New York service.

ADRIATIC AT SOUTHAMPTON

November 1934 sold for £65,000 to Japanese shipbreakers. The price of steel had risen sharply, the Japanese war machine needing fine grade steel. 5 March 1935 arrived at Osaka for breaking up.

LAURENTIC I (1909-1917): AT LIVERPOOL LANDING STAGE

Built by Harland & Wolff, Belfast. Laid down in 1907 as ALBERTA for the Dominion Line, transferred to White Star before launching in September 1908. Renamed LAURENTIC for the new White Star- Dominion Line Joint Service to Canada. Her propelling machinery of two 4 cylinder triple expansion engines, exhausting steam into a low pressure turbine, was to become a standard feature incorporated in most of the company's vessels. 29 April 1909 maiden voyage on the Liverpool-Quebec-Montreal service.

Sister ship: MEGANTIC

LAURENTIC IN THE ST. LAWRENCE

25 January 1917 sailing at full speed around the North coast of Ireland near Lough Swilley LAURENTIC hit two mines capsized and sank with the loss of 345 lives out of the 475 onboard. LAURENTIC's cargo included 3,211 gold bars part of Britain's payment for munitions supplied by the Canadian Government. February 1917 work began on recovering the gold, after an estimated 5,000 dives, 3,186 bars valued at £6.5 million were recovered by 1924.

MEGANTIC (1909-1931): & MAGNETIC IN THE MERSEY

Built by Harland & Wolff, Belfast. Laid down in 1908 as ALBANY for the Dominion Line. Transferred to White Star before launching in December. renamed MEGANTIC for the Canadian service. As part of an experiment fitted with conventional triple expansion engines, her sister fitted with triple expansions exhausting into a low pressure turbine. Sea trials proved her sister LAURENTIC faster and more economical to run.

Sister ship: LAURENTIC I

White Star Line, R.M.S. "Megantic" 14,878 tons, at Havana.

MEGANTIC AT HAVANA

During the 1920s slump in North Atlantic passenger travel White Star sent a number of their vessels cruising to the Mediterranean and West Indies.

ALTAR ONBOARD MEGANTIC

July 1931 laid up at Rothesay Bay. 1932 during a storm MEGANTIC broke her cables and had to be secured with the help of tugs. January 1933 sold to Japanese shipbreakers, broken up at Osaka.

"NORTHLAND"

ZEELAND (1910-1911)

Built by John Brown & Co., Clydebank for the Red Star Line as ZEELAND. 1910 transferred to White Star for the Liverpool-Boston service as replacement tonnage for REPUBLIC. 1915 renamed NORTHLAND to anglicize her German name. 1920 reverted to Red Star and renamed ZEELAND. 1927 sold to Atlantic Transport and renamed MINNESOTA. October 1929 sold to Thomas W. Ward Ltd., for scrapping. 1930 broken up at Inverkeithing, Firth of Forth.

OLYMPIC (1911-1935): ON THE STOCKS

Laid down at Harland & Wolff, Belfast on 16 December 1908 as Yard No. 400. Her sister TITANIC Yard No. 401 laid down on the adjacent slipway on the 31 March 1909 is still at the plating stage.

Sister ships: TITANIC & BRITANNIC II

OLYMPIC
BEFORE LAUNCHING

Preparations for the launch included painting the liner's hull white and fitting bracing bars to her rudder, the launching ways were covered with 15 tons of tallow, about 5 tons of tallow and train oil mixed and three tons of soap.

"LAUNCH OF THE OLYMPIC" AT BELFAST   20TH OCT., 1910.

COPYRIGHT PHOTO
A. R. HOGG. BELFAST.

OLYMPIC ENTERING THE RIVER LAGAN

20 October 1910 in the presence of the Lord Lieutenant of Ireland, the Countess of Aberdeen, J. Pierpont Morgan, J. Bruce Ismay and a number of distinguished guests OLYMPIC was launched. The liner took 62 seconds from the release of the hydraulic launching triggers to enter the water, reaching a maximum speed of 12.5 knots. Lord Pirrie supervised the launch assisted by Charles Payne shipyard manager, and Mr. R.F. Keith head foreman carpenter responsible for the practical work of launching all White Star's vessels.

BOW VIEW, "OLYMPIC" DOCKED IN NEW GRAVING DOCK, BELFAST 1ST APRIL 1911
DISPLACEMENT OF VESSEL. 33,000 TONS.

OLYMPIC IN THE GRAVING DOCK

1 April 1911 The Belfast Commissioner's new Graving Dock the largest in the world, was opened with the drydocking of OLYMPIC for final fitting out, cleaning and repainting. Between 3 and 4,000 men worked to complete the liner in time for her sea trials in May.

THE "OLYMPIC" AT SOUTHAMPTON AFTER THE COLLISION. 20 SEP. 1911. 5 ILK. 4.

OLYMPIC AFTER COLLISION WITH H.M.S. HAWKE

14 June 1911 maiden voyage on the Southampton-New York service. 20 September collided with H.M.S. HAWKE in the Solent. OLYMPIC's starboard quarter was badly holed above and below the water line, causing the cancellation of her voyage to New York. Repairs at Harland & Wolff lasted six weeks. At the subsequent inquiry OLYMPIC was held solely to blame for the collision. The Royal Navy successfully argued that OLYMPIC's great size and displacement had caused HAWKE's steering to jam as she tried to pass the liner's stern drawing the destroyer off course and causing her to ram OLYMPIC on the starboard side about 90ft. from the stern.

OLYMPIC LEAVING THE WHITE STAR DOCK, SOUTHAMPTON, 24 APRIL 1912

Nine days after the terrible disaster that overtook her sister, OLYMPIC left Southampton on her scheduled sailing to New York. October 1912 after the findings of the TITANIC inquiry were published OLYMPIC returned to Harland & Wolff, Belfast for extensive improvements and modifications costing £250,000. 1913 re-entered Southampton-New York service.

R. M. S. Olympic.

OLYMPIC AT SEA

September 1915 commissioned as H.M.T. OLYMPIC becoming a troop transport during the Dardanelles and Gallipoli campaigns. 12 May 1918 rammed and sank U-103 near the Lizard. August 1919 refitted by Harland & Wolff, Belfast and converted to oil firing reducing her engine room staff from 350 to just 60. 1930 redecorated and refurnished at a cost of £45,000. 1934 taken in to the new Cunard-White Star fleet. 16 May rammed and sank the Nantucket Lightship, a $500,000 claim was filed against the company by the U.S. Government. 27 March 1935 last voyage on the Southampton-New York service. September sold to Sir John Jarvis for £100,000. Resold to Thomas W. Ward Ltd., on the understanding that the liner was to be broken up at Jarrow-on-Tyne to relieve the serious unemployment in the North East of England. 13 October arrived at Palmer's old shipyard, Jarrow. The price of steel from OLYMPIC fetched just over £2. 3s. per ton.

ZEALANDIC TOWING GARTHSNAID 3·4·1923

ZEALANDIC (1911-1926): TOWING GARTHSNAID INTO PORT

Built by Harland & Wolff, Belfast in 1911 for the White Star-Shaw Savill & Albion Joint Service. 30 October maiden voyage Liverpool-Wellington. January 1913 sailed from New Zealand with a record cargo of wool. Chartered by the Western Australian Government as an emigrant carrier. 2 July 1915 while steaming in the English Channel narrowly escaped being torpedoed by a German U-Boat, using her higher speed to escape. July 1917 requisitioned by the British Government. June 1919 released back to her owners. April 1923 ZEALANDIC earned her owners an unexpected £6,350 salvage money bonus by taking under tow the disabled sailing ship GARTHSNAID off Cape Howe into Melbourne. June 1926 transferred on charter to the Aberdeen Line, renamed MAMILIUS, continuing on the Australian service from Liverpool. February 1934 sold to Shaw Savill & Albion, renamed MAMARI. 1939 sold to the British Admiralty, later converted into a dummy version of the aircraft carrier H.M.S. HERMES. 4 June 1941 beached and lost after German air attack near Cromer.

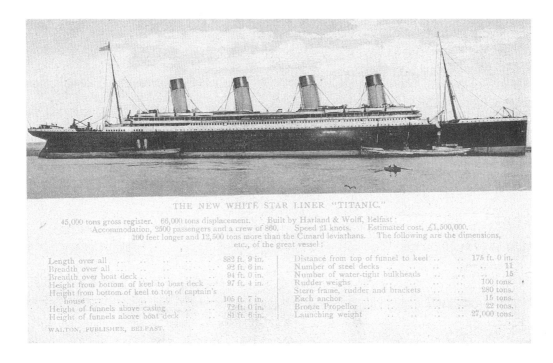

THE NEW WHITE STAR LINER "TITANIC."

45,000 tons gross register. 66,000 tons displacement. Built by Harland & Wolff, Belfast.
Accommodation, 2500 passengers and a crew of 860. Speed 21 knots. Estimated cost, £1,500,000.
100 feet longer and 12,500 tons more than the Cunard leviathans. The following are the dimensions,
etc., of the great vessel :

Length over all	882 ft. 9 in.	Distance from top of funnel to keel	175 ft. 0 in.
Breadth over all	92 ft. 6 in.	Number of steel decks	11
Breadth over boat deck	94 ft. 0 in.	Number of water-tight bulkheads	15
Height from bottom of keel to boat deck	97 ft. 4 in.	Rudder weighs	100 tons.
Height from bottom of keel to top of captain's		Stern frame, rudder and brackets	280 tons.
house	105 ft. 7 in.	Each anchor	15 tons.
Height of funnels above casing	72 ft. 0 in.	Bronze Propellor	22 tons.
Height of funnels above boat deck	81 ft. 6 in.	Launching weight	27,000 tons.

WALTON, PUBLISHER, BELFAST.

TITANIC (1912)

Laid down by Harland & Wolff, Belfast on the 31 March 1909 as Yard No. 401. 31 May 1911 launched at 12.15 p.m. and watched by an estimated 100,000 people. Later the same day her sister OLYMPIC was delivered to Liverpool.

Sister ships: **OLYMPIC & BRITANNIC II**

FAREWELL TO BELFAST.
DEPARTURE OF THE LARGEST VESSEL IN THE WORLD,
THE WHITE STAR LINER "TITANIC," 46,328 TONS. APRIL 3rd, 1912.

TITANIC LEAVING BELFAST

3 April 1912 after successfully completing her sea trials TITANIC left Belfast at 8 p.m. for Southampton.

TITANIC
AT THE WHITE STAR DOCK, SOUTHAMPTON

5 April, Good Friday and TITANIC is dressed overall in flags for the benefit of the people of Southampton.

WHITE STAR LINER TITANIC.
LENGTH 882 ft. 6 ins.   BREADTH 92 ft. 6 ins   45,000 TONNAGE.
SAILED FROM SOUTHAMPTON ON HER ILL-FATED MAIDEN VOYAGE ON APRIL 10TH, 1912. CARRYING 2,350 PASSENGERS AND CREW. STRUCK AN ICEBERG
OFF THE COAST OF NEWFOUNDLAND. PERISHED ON SUNDAY NIGHT APRIL 14TH, 1912

TITANIC LEAVING SOUTHAMPTON

10 April maiden voyage on the Southampton-New York service, carrying 180 first, 240 second and 494 third class passengers with 898 officers and crew.

White Star Liner
"TITANIC"
leaving SOUTHAMPTON
COPYRIGHT MAX MILLS.

TITANIC PASSING THE NEW YORK

TITANIC's great displacement almost caused her to collide firstly with OCEANIC (extreme left) her moorings straining almost to breaking point as she passed, and secondly with NEW YORK (behind TITANIC). The suction as she passed was so great that it broke the liner's moorings and a collision was only narrowly averted by reversing and then stopping TITANIC's engines, with tugs pushing the helpless NEW YORK back to her berth. Later the same day TITANIC called at Cherbourg and finally Queenstown leaving the Irish port on the 11 April at 11 p.m. her passenger list increased to 1,308.

"STEAMER TITANIC"
Largest and most luxurious in the World. Launched at Belfast Ireland, May 1911. Length 882 ft. 6 inches. Displacement 66,000 tons.
On her maiden trip struck a mammoth iceberg on Sunday, April 14th at 10.25 P. M. 41° 46 minutes, north latitude-50° 14 minutes, west longitude.
The worst disaster known in Marine History. Sunk at 2.20 A. M. April 15 1912, with a loss of over 1300 lives.

TITANIC 'IN MEMORIAM' POSTCARD

14 April at 11.30 p.m. steaming at 22 knots TITANIC's lookout in the crow's nest rang three bells and phoned the bridge; 'Iceberg right ahead'. In the next few minutes the liners engines were put full astern, her helm put hard-a-starboard, but the iceberg was too close and TITANIC hit the iceberg a glancing blow which opened up her first six water tight compartments to the sea. TITANIC sank at 2.20 a.m. with the loss of 1,503 lives due entirely to the shortage of lifeboats. This American postcard published shortly after the disaster has incorrect details on the sinking.

"Titanic" Engineers Memorial, Southampton.

TITANIC ENGINEERS MEMORIAL, SOUTHAMPTON

Unveiled on 22 April two years after the disaster, to the memory of all 36 TITANIC engineers who lost their lives. The memorial built of bronze and granite is situated in Southampton's East Park. Railings placed in front of the memorial after its unveiling were removed in 1940 to help with the war effort.

WHITE STAR LINE.

NEW TRIPLE-SCREW STEAMER "CERAMIC," 18,000 TONS, LARGEST STEAMER TO AUSTRALIA.

CERAMIC (1913-1934)

Built by Harland & Wolff, Belfast in 1912. July 1913 completed in time for the Royal Naval Review at Liverpool. CERAMIC designed for the Australian service, carried large numbers of that country's troops during the first world war.

158   Length, 674 feet.   R.M.S. "Ceramic."   Width, 69 feet.   Tonnage, 18,481.

CERAMIC AT SEA

August 1934 ownership of CERAMIC passed to Shaw Savill & Albion after White Star's merger with Cunard. December 1942 torpedoed and sunk by U-515, west of the Azores. A total of 655 lives were lost, the German U-Boat rescued one survivor as proof of their kill.

LAPLAND (1914-1919)

Built by Harland & Wolff, Belfast in 1908 for Red Star as LAPLAND. October 1914 transferred to White Star for the Liverpool-New York service. April 1917 mined in Liverpool Bay, reaching port under her own power. November 1919 last voyage for White Star returned to Red Star. October 1933 sold to Japanese shipbreakers for £29,000. November broken up at Osaka.

12. Harland and Wolff's Shipyard, Belfast

BRITANNIC II (1915-1916): ON THE STOCKS

Laid down by Harland & Wolff, Belfast in November 1911 as Yard No. 433. Built on the same slipway as her sister OLYMPIC. Major alterations undertaken after the findings of the TITANIC inquiry. Complete inner skin fitted giving the liner 2ft. extra beam than her sisters. All 16 bulkheads heightened and gantry davits fitted to allow the launching of lifeboats from either side of the ship despite the builders claim however this was a physical impossibility due to the position of her funnels.

Sister ships: OLYMPIC & TITANIC

LAUNCH OF THE R. M. S. "BRITANNIC", AT BELFAST, 26th Feb. 1914.
LENGTH OVER ALL: 900 FEET.   BREADTH: 94 FEET.
HEIGHT (FROM KEEL TO NAVIGATING BRIDGE): 104 FT. 6 INS.
GROSS TONNAGE: 50,000 TONS.   PASSENGER ACCOMMODATION: 2,600
CREW ACCOMMODATION: 950

BRITANNIC LEAVING THE WAYS

26 February 1914 launched. The last vessel of the Olympic Class and the largest British built liner until the advent of the QUEEN MARY in 1935.

THIS IS A REAL PHOTO

BRITANNIC ENTERING THE RIVER LAGAN

170 tons of anchor chain brought the 24,800 ton hull to a standstill after 81 seconds. 2 July White Star announced that BRITANNIC would not enter the Southampton-New York mail service until the spring of 1915. September dry-docked to receive her propellers.

Models of WHITE STAR Steamers "BRITANNIC" 5,000 tons, built in 1874,
and "BRITANNIC," 50,000 tons, built in 1914.

BUILDERS MODELS OF BRITANNIC I & II

13 November 1915 requisitioned by the British Government. 6 December Germany informed of BRITANNIC's status as a hospital ship. 8 December sea trials held in Belfast Lough, fitted out for hospital ship service and repainted in International Red Cross colours. 23 December maiden voyage Liverpool-Murdos under the command of Captain Charles A. Bartlett.

H.M.H.S. BRITANIC

H.M.H.S. BRITANNIC
21 November 1916 while steaming in the Aegean Sea four miles west of Port St. Nikolo in the Zea Channel BRITAN-NIC was struck by a mine or torpedo, exploding on her starboard side about 150 ft. from the bow. The liner was racked by violent explosions later believed to have been coal dust exploding in her bunkers, causing massive damage and disabling the automatic system for shutting the water tight doors. The liner sank in just under an hour with the loss of 21 lives. 4 July 1919 Harland & Wolff held a sale of interior fittings and furniture from the liner.

.RED STAR LINE, S/S. "BELGENLAND." 27,200 Tons Triple Screw

BELGIC IV (1917-1921)

Built by Harland & Wolff, Belfast for Red Star. 31 December 1914 launched as BELGENLAND II. Building work suspended, priority given to naval construction. Completion as a fast merchant cargo vessel ordered by the Shipping Controller. 21 June 1917 handed over to White Star management, renamed BELGIC IV with only two funnels and no top hamper. 4 April 1923 reverted to Red Star after completion to original design, renamed BELGENLAND. January 1935 sold to the Atlantic Transport Co., West Virginia, renamed COLUMBIA. 1936 sold to P. & W. MacLellan Ltd., for scrapping at Bo'ness, Firth of Forth.

S.16814.

WHITE STAR LINE S. S. "VEDIC."

VEDIC (1918-1934)

Built by Harland & Wolff at their Govan yards in 1918. Towed from Glasgow to Belfast to have her engines fitted. These were the first geared turbines built by the company. June 1918 operated under the British Government Liner Requisition Scheme. Returned to White Star, first commercial voyage 28 December 1919. 1920 refitted at Middlesbrough for the Canadian emigrant trade with accommodation for 1,250 third class passengers only. 1934 sold to Scottish shipbreakers for £10,400 after remaining idle since 1930. Broken up at Rosyth, Firth of Forth.

S.S. "CLAN COLQUHOUN"

GALLIC II (1918-1933)

Built by Workman Clark & Co., Belfast as WAR ARGUS a standard 'G' type cargo vessel for the Shipping Controller in 1918 sailing under White Star management. Twenty two vessels of this type were built. January 1920 purchased by White Star, renamed GALLIC II and placed on the Australian service. 1933 sold to Clan Line for £53,000, renamed CLAN COLQUHOUN. June 1956 broken up at Hong Kong.

Wreck of SS "Bardic"

BARDIC (1919–1925): ON THE STAG ROCK

Built by Harland & Wolff, Belfast in 1918 for the Shipping Controller named WAR PRIAM a 'G' type cargo vessel. 13 March 1919 purchased by White Star and renamed BARDIC for the Liverpool-New York service. Operated by Atlantic Transport from June 1919 until April 1921. Reverted to White Star for the Australian service. 31 August 1924 stranded while on passage Liverpool-London on the Stag Rock, Lizard.

701 Salved S.S. Bardic at Falmouth. opie.

BARDIC SALVED IN FALMOUTH HARBOUR

After being ashore for a month BARDIC was refloated, towed to Falmouth, and beached for temporary repairs. While she underwent drydock repairs at Belfast her Captain Charles Greame was killed in a express train crash between Liverpool and Birkenhead. 1925 sold to the Aberdeen Line for a book value of £242,086, renamed HORATIUS. 3 August 1932 transferred to Shaw Savill & Albion, renamed KUMARA. 1937 sold to J. Latsis, Piraeus renamed MARATHON. November 1941 sunk by the SCHARNHORST North-East of Cape Verde.

"MOBILE"

MOBILE (1920)

Built by Blohm & Voss, Hamburg in 1909 for Hamburg American Line as CLEVELAND. Laid up throughout the war, surrendered March 1919 became U.S. Transport MOBILE. Chartered by White Star for two return voyages Liverpool-New York. 1920 sold to Byron Steamship Co., London renamed King Alexander. 1923 sold to United-American Lines renamed CLEVELAND. 1926 sold back to Hamburg American without name change. 1931 laid up at Hamburg, scrapped in 1933.

S.S. HAVERFORD LIVERPOOL.

HAVERFORD (1921-1924)

Built by John Brown & Co., Clydebank for the American Line as a sister to the MERION. Having survived stranding in May 1913 and three torpedo attacks during the war, ownership of HAVERFORD passed to White Star in 1921, sailing on the Liverpool-Philadelphia service. 1924 sold to Italian shipbreakers for £29,000, and broken up one year later.

S.S. Arabic.

ARABIC III (1921-1931)

Built by A.G. Weser, Bremen in 1908 for Norddeutsher Lloyd as BERLIN. During the war laid mine field which sank the British battleship AUDACIOUS. December 1919 surrendered to Britain as a war prize. Managed by P. & O. as a troop transport to India. November 1920 sold to White Star renamed ARABIC III and refitted at Portsmouth Dockyard. 1925 transferred to Red Star for the Antwerp-New York service. 1930 reverted to White Star. July laid up. December 1931 sold for scrapping at Genoa realising £17,500.

HOMERIC (1922-1935)

Launched on the 17 December 1913 by F. Schichau, Danzig, for Norddeutsher Lloyd as COLUMBUS. August 1914 following the outbreak of hostilities construction work on the 80% completed liner halted. 28 June 1919 the Treaty of Versailles stipulated that COLUMBUS should be handed over to the British Government as a war prize. June 1920 offered for sale. Purchased by White Star, renamed HOMERIC. Building work continued at Danzig under the supervision of Harland & Wolff.

Sister ship: COLUMBUS ex-HINDENBURG (Renamed in 1924 after the surrender of her sister to Britain).

CONTROL ROOM.

HOMERIC ENGINE CONTROL ROOM

21 January 1922 arrived at Southampton following her sea trials. 15 February maiden voyage on the Southampton-Cherbourg-New York express service, the largest twin screw reciprocating engine ship in the world. HOMERIC's intermediate speed of 18 knots meant she was always falling behind schedule. October 1923 converted by Harland & Wolff, Belfast to oil firing, passenger accommodation altered and improved. April 1924 returned to service with a one knot increase in speed to 19.5 knots, this reduced her Atlantic crossing time by 24 hours. 1930 altered accommodation for 523 first, 841 second and 314 third class passengers.

1165. C. R. Hoffmann,
Southampton.

White Star Line R.M.S. "HOMERIC"
First Class Dining Saloon.

34,356 Tons.

HOMERIC: 1ST. CLASS DINING SALOON

1 June 1932 last voyage on the Southampton-New York service. Transferred to permanent cruising work with altered accommodation for 472 first, 832 tourist and 659 third class passengers.

S.17731 WHITE STAR LINE R.M.S. "HOMERIC" 34,351 TONS.
THIRD CLASS GENERAL ROOM.

HOMERIC: 3RD. CLASS GENERAL ROOM

1934 taken into the new Cunard-White Star fleet. 28 September 1935 last commercial voyage from Southampton on a 21 day cruise of the Mediterranean. On return laid up at Ryde off the Isle of Wight and offered for sale. 27 February 1936 sold to Thomas W. Ward Ltd., Shipbreakers for £74,000. March arrived at Inverkeithing for breaking up.

R.M.S. MAJESTIC.

MAJESTIC II (1922-1936)

Laid down by Blohm & Voss, Hamburg in April 1913 for the Hamburg Amerika Line. 20 June 1914 launched by Countess Hanna von Bismarck, and named after her late grandfather Chancellor Bismarck. August work suspended for the duration of the hostilities, most internal brass and copper fittings stripped for the War effort. 28 June 1919 Germany signed the Treaty of Versailles, also agreeing to a four word financial condition; 'reparation for damage done'. The interpretation of what was meant by these four words proved a major point of argument during the Treaty negotiations. BISMARCK only surrendered to the Reparations Commission after lengthy legal wrangling. Building work recommenced on the partially complete liner lying in the River Elbe under British Government supervision. 5 October 1920 completion considerably delayed by fire, sabotage suspected but never proved.

Sister ships: **BERENGARIA ex-IMPERATOR & LEVIATHAN ex-VATERLAND**

1ST CLASS ENTRANCE B. DECK, R. M. S. MAJESTIC.

MAJESTIC : 1ST. CLASS ENTRANCE, B DECK

February 1921 BISMARCK and her sister IMPERATOR (already under Cunard management) were offered to White Star and Cunard. The two companies to avoid outbidding each other purchased the liners jointly, a joint ownership that last ten years. Cunard wished to keep IMPERATOR renaming her BERENGARIA while management of BISMARCK passed to White Star. Completion of the liner and conversion to oil firing supervised by Harland & Wolff. 10 April 1922 successfully completed sea trials, renamed MAJESTIC. 10 May maiden voyage on the Southampton-New York service as the largest liner in the world. August inspected by King George V and Queen Mary during Cowes week. Whilst the King was onboard the Royal Standard flew from MAJESTIC's main mast, an exceptional honour for the ship and the White Star Line.

MAJESTIC IN THE FLOATING DRYDOCK, SOUTHAMPTON

January 1924 ran aground on the Isle of Wight coast without serious damage. June while on an eastbound crossing MAJESTIC steamed at 25.91 knots for 24 hours. January 1928 refitted by Harland & Wolff at Southampton. New Boilers fitted and the black tops of her funnels were deepened. 1932 joint ownership of MAJESTIC and BERENGARIA by White Star and Cunard ended. 1934 taken into the new Cunard-White Star fleet.

S.S. "MAJESTIC" IN KING GEORGE V. GRAVING DOCK.
LARGEST GRAVING DOCK IN THE WORLD.

36 A

MAJESTIC IN THE KING GEORGE V GRAVING DOCK

19 January first liner to use the King George V Graving Dock, Southampton. 13 February 1936 last voyage on the Southampton-New York service. 15 May purchased by Thomas W. Ward for £115,000. To ease her passage under the Forth Railway Bridge her three funnels and two masts were cut down. July due to a clause in the sales contract MAJESTIC could not be resold except for scrap. The Admiralty exchanged twenty four old warships amounting to the same tonnage. Handed over to John I. Thorneycroft, Southampton for conversion to a training ship for 1,500 Cadets and 500 Artificer apprentices, renamed H.M.S. CALEDONIA conversion work costing £472,000. September 1939 refitted as a transport planned by the Admiralty, fire broken out onboard CALEDONIA sinking on an even keel in shallow water. March 1940 resold to Ward's and broken up on the spot down to the waterline. 17 July 1943 the remainder of the wreck raised and towed five miles to Ward's yard at Inverkeithing for final demolition.

PITTSBURGH (1922-1925)

Laid down by Harland & Wolff, Belfast in 1913 for the American Line as PITTSBURGH. August 1914 work suspended for the duration of the war. 1922 completed as an oil burner for White Star running on the Liverpool-Philadelphia-Boston service as a consort for HAVERFORD. January 1925 sailed for Red Star on the Antwerp-Southampton-Cherbourg-New York service. 1926 renamed PENNLAND II. February 1935 sold to Arnold Bernstein's Red Star Line, Hamburg. April 1938 sold to Holland-America Line. 1 August 1940 requisitioned by the British Military of War Transport, fitted out as a troop transport. 25 April 1941 bombed seven times and sunk by the Luftwaffe in the Gulf of Athens.

Sister ships: REGINA & DORIC II

RED STAR LINE.

TRIPLE-SCREW "PENNLAND"
(EX-PITTSBURGH)
16.332 TONS.

107

WHITE STAR LINER
TWIN-SCREW S.S. "DORIC," 16,484 TONS

DORIC II (1923-1935)

Built by Harland & Wolff, Belfast laid down in 1921 but not completed until 1923 due to financial difficulties within IMMCO. DORIC was the only White Star vessel to be powered by turbines alone. She spent most of her life cruising primarily to the Mediterranean. Surviving the amalgamation of Cunard and White Star in 1934, her days were numbered. September 1935 collided with the French liner FORMIGNY, the new company decided she was not worth repairing and sold her for scrapping to John Cashmore Ltd., for £35,000 a fraction of what she had cost to build 12 years before.

Sister ships: **REGINA & PITTSBURGH**

REGINA (1925-1929)

Built 1913 by Harland & Wolff, Glasgow for Dominion Line. April 1917 completed as a transport. Finished to original design in 1920 for the White Star-Dominion Joint Service. 1925 repainted as a White Star liner (as illustrated) on the disappearance of the Dominion Line. December 1929 transferred to Red Star. 1930 renamed WESTERNLAND II. February 1935 purchased by Arnold Bernstein's Red Star Line. 1938 purchased by Holland-America Line. 1 August requisitioned by the Ministry of Transport, fitted out as a troop transport. February 1943 purchased by the Ministry of War Transport handed over to the Admiralty for conversion to a destroyer repair ship. October 1946 sold to Christian Salvesen, Leith for conversion to a whale factory ship, plan abandoned. 15 July 1947 sold for scrap.

Sister ships: **PITTSBURGH & DORIC II**

ALBERTIC (1927-1933)

Laid down by A. G. Weser, Bremen in 1913 for Norddeutsher Lloyd as MUNCHEN. June 1919 designated by the Treaty of Versailles as War Reparations, transferred to Britain while still on the stocks. 27 March 1923 transferred to Royal Mail after successfully completely sea trails, renamed OHIO. 1927 sold to White Star renamed ALBERTIC. 193? laid up at Holy Loch. July 1934 sold for £34,000 to Japanese shipbreakers, broken up at Osaka.

1133 C. R. Hoffmann, Southampton.   S. S. CALGARIC.   16.063 Tons.

CALGARIC (1927-1933)

Built by Harland & Wolff, Belfast in 1918 for the Pacific Steam Navigation Company as ORCA. Completed as a cargo vessel without passenger accommodation for the Shipping Controller. 1921 completed at Belfast to original design. 1923 transferred to Royal Mail. 1927 sold to White Star renamed CALGARIC for Liverpool-Quebec-Montreal service. Spent long periods as a reserve steamer laid up at Milford Haven after holiday cruises. 1934 after the amalgamation of Cunard and White Star sold for £31,000. December broken up at Inverkeithing.

S.288.   R.M.S. "LAURENTIC."

LAURENTIC II (1927-1938)

Built by Harland & Wolff, Belfast in 1927 for the Canadian service. The only White Star liner built to a fixed price and the company's last coal burner. 1934 taken into the amalgamated Cunard and White Star fleets. July 1935 rammed by the NAPIER STAR off the Skerries in the Irish Sea with the loss of six lives. September 1939 converted to an Armed Merchant Cruiser with seven 5.5 inch guns and three 4.0 inch Anti Aircraft guns. 3 November 1940 torpedoed four times and sunk with the loss of 49 lives off the Bloody Foreland by U-99 commanded by Otto Kretschmer, Germany's most famous U-Boat 'Ace'.

"M.V. BRITANNIC"   JUNE 1930

BRITANNIC III (1930-1960): AT LIVERPOOL LANDING STAGE

Built by Harland & Wolff, Belfast. White Star's first motor vessel, powered by two 10 cylinder double-acting diesel engines producing 13,000 ihp each. 28 June 1930 BRITANNIC left Liverpool on her maiden voyage for New York via Belfast and Glasgow.

Sister ship: GEORGIC II

BRITANNIC AT COTE D'AZUR

1934 taken into the amalgamated Cunard and White Star fleets, retaining her White Star colours. April 1935 began new London-Le Havre-Southampton-New York service. 1936 BRITANNIC along with GEORGIC became the last White Star liners in service.

BRITANNIC AT LIVERPOOL LANDING STAGE

August 1939 requisitioned and converted to a transport for 3,000 troops. During the war she carried 180,000 troops and steamed a total of 376,000 miles. 1947 refitted and returned to Cunard-White Star service. 4 December 1960 sold to British Iron & Steel Co. 1961 scrapped by Thomas W. Ward Ltd., at Inverkeithing.

M.V. "GEORGIC."

GEORGIC II (1932-1955): IN THE MERSEY

Built by Harland & Wolff, Belfast in 1931 for White Star's Liverpool-New York service. 25 June 1932 maiden voyage to New York, arrived 12 hours ahead of schedule. Taken into the new Cunard-White Star fleet. April 1935 first voyage on the new London-Le Havre-Southampton-New York service with BRITANNIC. The two sisters were the largest liners to use the Port of London.

Sister ship: BRITANNIC III

GEORGIC SHOWING BOMB DAMAGE

March 1940 requisitioned by the British Government and converted on the Clyde into a troop transport for 3,000 men.
14 July 1941 bombed and sunk by the Luftwaffe at Port Tewfik on the southern end of the Suez Canal. October salvage
experts were called in to raise the liner, it was found that the propelling machinery could be cleaned and brought back
into service. December towed to Port Sudan for temporary repairs. March 1942 towed to Karachi for further repairs.
11 December left Karachi under her own steam for Belfast via the Cape of Good Hope. 1943-1944 rebuilt by Harland &
Wolff as a transport with only one funnel and mast.

GEORGIC AFTER RECONSTRUCTION

September 1948 refitted by Palmers' & Co., Hebburn on the Tyne for the Australian and New Zealand trade as a one class emigrant carrier with accommodation for 1,962 passengers. Returned to service and still in White Star colours under charter to Cunard. 19 November 1955 last commercial voyage ended at Liverpool, laid up and offered for sale. January 1956 sold for scrapping. February broken up by Shipbreaking Industries Ltd., Faslane.

WHITE STAR SAILING SHIPS

"BROUGHTON" ADAMSON, ROTAFSRY.

BROUGHTON (1868-1876)

The first ship built by Harland & Wolff, Belfast for White Star, predating the ordering of OCEANIC I by two years. A half share in BROUGHTON was taken up by Edward Harland, Gustav Wolff and his uncle Gustav C. Schwabe whose house Broughton Hall in West Derby, the sailing ship was named after. 1876 sold to William Thomas & Co., Swansea. 1899 sold to Norwegian owners. December 1902 wrecked while on passage from Hamburg to the Clyde.

(No 6.)
WHITE STAR TRAINING SHIP "MERSEY", DURING THE KINGS VISIT TO L'POOL.

MERSEY (1908-1914): TRAINING SHIP

The policy of White Star's owners was the training of cadets under sail. 1908, J. Bruce Ismay purchased a 1,713 ton steel hulled sailing ship, built on the Clyde in 1894, by Chas. Connell & Company, Glasgow. Renamed MERSEY sailing under the command of Captain F.W. Corner, as an ocean going classroom for sixty cadets. MERSEY had the distinction of being the first sailing vessel to carry wireless. August 1908 made the first of six return voyages to Australia, carrying cargo outward and homeward bound. The first voyage was made around the Cape to Sydney, in just under three months, and homeward around Cape Horn. After her arrival in the Thames the Board of Trade set examinations for the cadets, the results were not only satisfactory, but contained many favourable comments to those responsible for the scheme. This postcard shows the MERSEY dressed with flags overall for King George V and Queen Mary's visit to Liverpool in July 1913 to open another section of the Gladstone Dock system. September 1914 planned voyage to Australia cancelled as her captain, officers and cadets were required for war service. November sold by White Star's chairman Harold Sanderson.

WHITE STAR BUILDINGS & DOCKS

WHITE STAR OFFICES, LIVERPOOL

The White Star Line's headquarters were based at 30 James Street, Liverpool. Designed by the architect Richard Norman Shaw in 1894 for a fee of £1952 8s 6d, the building was an improved version of Scotland Yard, his earlier work for London's Metropolitan Police. With the building completed in 1895, White Star moved out of it's smaller offices at 10 Water Street, Liverpool the same year. The company's headquarters remained at James Street until 1927, when it transferred to Royal Mail House, Leadenhall Street, London after it's acquisition by the Royal Mail Group. The building was badly damaged by the Luftwaffe during World War II, but was later restored to its former glory.

OCEANIC HOUSE, LONDON

The acquisition of White Star by IMMCO brought so many changes to the company's operations that the need arose for larger and more prestigious offices in London, to handle the extra volume of work caused by running effectively six shipping lines under one roof. The decision was made for new offices to be designed by Henry Tanner Jnr., and to be built in the heart of London's West End. By the spring of 1903, Oceanic House 1 Cockspur Street, SW1 near Trafalgar Square was opened to the public. To help celebrate the coronation of George V in June 1911, and the maiden voyage of OLYMPIC during the same month, the facade of Oceanic House was decorated with an illuminated half model of OLYMPIC, a giant white star and the letter G.R., the rest of the building covered with similarly illuminated smaller stars, British and American flags and over 3000 lights. November 1932 the headquarters of White Star Line Limited were transferred from the Royal Mail's offices in Leadenhall Street to Oceanic House. 1934 with the amalgamation of Cunard and White Star the building became surplus to requirements and was sold.

F. G. O. Stuart. No. 2123   WHITE STAR DOCK, SOUTHAMPTON

WHITE STAR DOCK, SOUTHAMPTON

1909 work began on building a new enlarged dock at Southampton for White Star's new giants OLYMPIC, TITANIC and BRITANNIC II. In 1907 the company transferred its express service from Liverpool to Southampton and decided to further improve its New York service with the new Olympic Class liners. The London and South-Western Railway keen to improve the docks and keep its largest customer happy, set about extensive alterations, with the erection of four huge cargo and passenger sheds one of which was 700 ft. x 120 ft. wide. The dock itself in the shape of a parallelogram, measured 1,700 ft. x 400 ft. wide. Depth at low water was 40 ft., and at high water 53 ft., so the new giants could safely dock at any time without danger of touching bottom. Renamed Ocean Dock in the early 1920s, after the transfer of much of Cunard's passenger business to the port, the dock survives to this day. From left to right; OLYMPIC, ST. PAUL, AQUITANIA & MAURETANIA.

123

At the White Star Wharf Queenstown

WHITE STAR LINE WHARF, QUEENSTOWN

James Scott & Company were White Star's agents at Queenstown (now Cobh). This postcard shows passengers ready to leave by the tenders GLASGOW and IRELAND for one of the company's steamers that regularly moored in the deeper waters of Cork harbour.

NEW GANTRIES, HARLAND & WOLFFS, BELFAST.   RELIABLE SERIES 95 / 184

HARLAND & WOLFF GANTRIES, BELFAST

When Harland & Wolff received the go-ahead for the construction of the new Olympic Class liners from the White Star Line, they set about reorganising and modernising their Queen's Island yard. The company designed the gantries themselves but contracted Sir William Arrol & Company Ltd., Glasgow to construct them in an area that three slipways had formally occupied. The new gantries when completed covered an area of 840 ft. x 240 ft. and the height of one of the overhead cranes was 214 ft. In this early postcard of the gantries the newly laid keel of the OLYMPIC (yard No. 400) can be seen on the right, next to her work on TITANIC (Yard No. 401) had yet to begin.

"WHITE STAR"

LINE OF BRITISH & AUSTRALIAN EX-ROYAL MAIL PACKETS,

COMPRISING THE FOLLOWING MAGNIFICENT AND CELEBRATED CLIPPERS:

MORNING LIGHT,
RED JACKET,
WHITE STAR,
BLUE JACKET,
MISTRESS OF THE SEAS,
QUEEN of the NORTH,
LORD RAGLAN,
CHARIOT OF FAME,
GREAT AUSTRALIA,
WHITE JACKET,
SHALIMAR,
MERCHANT PRINCE,

MERMAID,
EMPIRE OF PEACE,
ELECTRIC,
TELEGRAPH,
SIROCCO,
BEN NEVIS,
ALFRED,
ARABIAN,
MIRIAM,
SHAFTESBURY,
GLEN DEVON,
OCEAN HOME,

Sailing on the 1st and 20th of every Month between

LIVERPOOL & MELBOURNE,

FORWARDING PASSENGERS TO

GEELONG, SYDNEY, ADELAIDE, & LAUNCESTON,

AT SHIP'S EXPENSE,

And Landing Passengers and their Luggage at the Wharf,—FREE OF CHARGE.

PACKET OF THE 20th OF DECEMBER, 1862,

IN THIS INSTANCE TO SAIL 22nd DECEMBER,

THE CELEBRATED CLIPPER SHIP

SOUTHERN EMPIRE,

1417 TONS REGISTER, 3000 TONS BURTHEN:

Loading on the West Side of Queen's Dock.

DIETARY SCALES and PASSAGE FARES,... Page 2 | LUGGAGE and PASSAGES of SHIPS,..........Page 3
REQUIREMENTS and SUBSTITUTES,............ 2 | DESCRIPTION of SHIP,............................. „ 4
Cash Orders on Melbourne from £1 and upwards Granted Free of Charge.

For Terms of Freight or Passage apply to H. T. WILSON & CHAMBERS, 21, Water Street, Liverpool; or to

CHARLES MOORE,

Government Agent, Cambridge Place, BATH.

(vertical left margin): CASH ORDERS ON MELBOURNE FROM £1 AND UPWARDS GRANTED FREE OF CHARGE.

"WHITE STAR" LINE OF BRITISH & AUSTRALIAN EX-ROYAL MAIL PACKETS — SAILING BILL (1862)

It is not hard to understand why Thomas H. Ismay bought the White Star house flag for his new company, when in the past it had flown over some of the most famous clippers ships of the day.

BRITANNIC I (1874-1902): 1ST. CLASS PASSENGER LIST

On BRITANNIC's voyage from New York to Liverpool in September 1885, under the command of Captain Hamilton Perry commodore of the line, she carried 74 passengers in her first class accommodation. Her surgeon on this voyage was Dr. William F.N. O'Loughlin, drowned twenty seven years later in the TITANIC disaster.

WHITE STAR LINE
ADVERTISING POSTER c. 1926

HOMERIC (1922-1935):
ADVERTISING POSTER c. 1922

WHITE STAR LINE —
RED STAR LINE S.S. ARABIC
BROCHURE COVER.

WHITE STAR LINE —
WHITE STAR-DOMINION
LINE BROCHURE COVER.

MAJESTIC II (1922-1936): 1ST-CLASS MENU COVER

MAJESTIC's cuisine was legendary on the North Atlantic, this seven course dinner menu for Thursday, July 13, 1933 included the following section from a choice of 88 different dishes;

Grape Fruit Cocktail

Potage Gombos

Poached Halibut, Sauce Cardinal

Noisettes of Lamb, St. Germain

Turkey, Sausage, Cranberry Sauce
French Beans   Garfield Potatoes

Peach Sabaynon

Dessert   Coffee

WHITE STAR LINE.
R.M.S. "MAJESTIC".

MAJESTIC II (1922-1936): ADVERTISING POSTCARD

One of the finest illustrations ever undertaken of MAJESTIC was by the famous poster artist Walter Thomas. The exaggeration of scale was a popular device by artists to try and impress would be passengers.

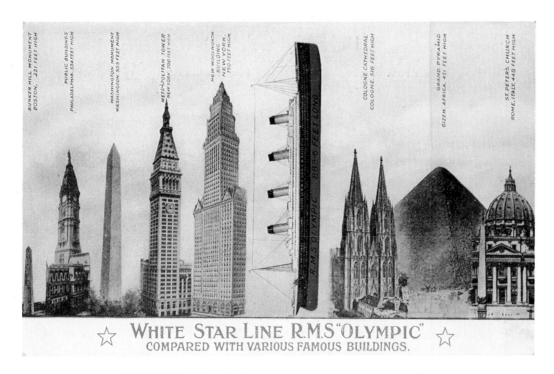

BUNKER HILL MONUMENT
BOSTON, 221 FEET HIGH

PUBLIC BUILDINGS
PHILADELPHIA, 534 FEET HIGH

WASHINGTON MONUMENT
WASHINGTON, 555 FEET HIGH

METROPOLITAN TOWER
NEW YORK, 700 FEET HIGH

NEW WOOLWORTH
BUILDING
NEW YORK,
750 FEET HIGH

R.M.S OLYMPIC   882·6 FEET LONG

COLOGNE CATHEDRAL
COLOGNE, 516 FEET HIGH

GRAND PYRAMID
GIZEH, AFRICA, 451 FEET HIGH

ST. PETER'S CHURCH
ROME, ITALY, 448 FEET HIGH

☆ WHITE STAR LINE R.M.S "OLYMPIC" ☆
COMPARED WITH VARIOUS FAMOUS BUILDINGS.

OLYMPIC (1911-1935): ADVERTISING POSTCARD

The White Star Line publicity department in Liverpool tried various methods to get across the size of OLYMPIC to the travelling public. This novel idea (illustrated) proved so successful that it was employed for many years on postcards, brochures and posters.

SELECT BIBLIOGRAPHY

ANDERSON, Roy, *White Star*, T. Stephenson & Sons Ltd., Prescot, Lancashire, 1964.

BEAUMONT, J.C.H., *Ships & People*, Geoffrey Bles, London, 1930

BEESLEY, Lawrence, *The Loss of the R.M.S. Titanic : Its Story & its Lessons*, William Heinemann, London, 1912.

BELLOWS, W., *The Ocean Liners of the World*, Kegan Paul, Trench, Trubner & Co. Ltd., London 1896.

BONSOR, N.P., *North Atlantic Seaway*, T. Stephenson & Sons Ltd., Prescot, Lancashire, 1955.

BOWYER, George W., *''Lively Ahoy''*, H.B. Broadbere, Southampton, 1930.

COREY, Lewis, *The House of Morgan*, G. Howard Watt, London, 1930.

CORAL, Thomas A., *A Book About Travelling Past & Present*, William P. Nimmo, London, 1877.

DUNN, Lawrence, *Famous Liners of the Past, Belfast Built*, Adlard Coles Ltd., London, 1964.

FINCH, Vernon E.W., *The Red Star Line*, De Branding N.V., Antwerp, 1988.

FLETCHER, R.A., *Steam-Ships: The History of their Development to the Present Day*, Sidgwick & Jackson Ltd., London, 1910. — *Travelling Palaces*, Sir Isaac Pitman & Sons Ltd., London, 1913.

GREEN, Edwin **& MOSS,** Michael, *A Business of National Importance: The Royal Mail Shipping Group 1902-1937*, Methuen & Co. Ltd., London, 1982.

HAYES, Sir Bertram, *Hull Down*, Cassell & Co. Ltd., London, 1925.

HOOD, A.G., Editor, *Souvenir Number of ''The Shipbuilder'' - The White Star Triple-Screw Atlantic Liners ''Olympic'' & ''Titanic''*, The Shipbuilder Press, Newcastle-on- Tyne & London, 1911.

HOYT, Edwin P., *The House of Morgan*, Frederick Warne & Co., London, N.D.

ISHERWOOD, J.H., *Steamers of the Past*, Sea Breezes, Liverpool, 1966.

JONES, Clement, *Pioneer Shipowners*, The Journal of Commerce & Shipping Telegraph, Liverpool, 1935.

KERSEY, H. Maitland, *Over the Oceans for 600,000 Miles*, The Alden Press, Oxford, Private Circulation, N.D.

LIGHTOLLER, Charles E., *Titanic & Other Ships*, Ivor Nicholson & Watson Ltd., London, 1935.

MAGINNIS, Arthur J., *The Atlantic Ferry*, Whittaker & Co., 1892.

MARTIN, Simon, *The Other Titanic*, David & Charles, Newton Abbot, Devon, 1980.

MAXTONE-GRAHAM, John, *The North Atlantic Run: ''The Only Way to Cross''*, Cassell & Co. Ltd., 1972.

MILSON, C.H., *The Coal was there for Burning*, Marine Media Management Ltd., London, 1975.
MOSS, Michael & **HUME,** John R., *Shipbuilders to the World: 125 Years of Harland & Wolff, Belfast 1861- 1986*, The Blackstaff Press, Belfast, Northern Ireland, 1986.

OLDHAM, Wilton J., *The Ismay Line*, Charles Birchall & Sons Ltd., Liverpool, 1961.

PARKER, Walter H., *Leaves from an Unwritten Log- Book*, Sampson Low, Marston & Co. Ltd., London, N.D.

SANDERSON, Basil, *Ships & Sealing Wax*, William Heinemann Ltd., London, 1967.
SAINT, Andrew, *Richard Norman Shaw*, Yale University Press, London, 1976.

TALBOT, Frederick A., *The Steamship Conquest of the World*, William Heinemann, London, 1912.

WATERS, Sydney D., *Shaw Savill Line — One Hundred Years of Trading*, Whitcombe & Tombs Ltd., London, 1961.
WHITE STAR LINE, *The White Star Royal Mail Steamship "Teutonic" (H.M. Armed Cruiser) at the Naval Review Spithead, June 26, 1897*, Stas. Walery & Co., London, 1898. Printed for private circulation only.

SHIP SPECIFICATIONS & INDEX

EXPLANATION

1. Roman numerals following a ship's name indicate that she is the first, second, third etc., vessel to carry that name in the fleet.

2. Dimensions are registered length × width × depth, vessels dimensions marked with an asterisk indicate overall Length. For ease of reference all dimensions are rounded off to the nearest foot.

3. Gross tonnage is shown as completed or as rebuilt (see note 7). It should be noted that these figures vary by subsequent modifications or changes to the measurement rules.

4. Engine types are indicated as follows;
   Reciprocating
   C = compound; T = triple expansion; Q = quadruple expansion.
   Turbine
   LPT = low pressure turbine; Tur = steam turbine.
   Diesel
   D = diesel.
   A plus sign indicates combination machinery.

5. Screws. The number of screws are shown thus; 1XS, 2XS etc.

6. Speed. The average speed obtained in White Star Line service is quoted in knots.

7. Rebuilt. In the case of ships substantially modified during their careers amended details appear immediately below their first entry.

Name	Dimensions	Tonnage	Machinery	Speed	Page
ADRIATIC I	* 452 × 41 × 31	3,868	C 1XS	14.00	3-4
ADRIATIC II	* 729 × 76 × 53	24,541	Q 2XS	17.00	60-61
AFRIC	* 565 × 63 × 40	11,948	Q 2XS	13.50	22
ALBERTIC	591 × 72 × 37	18,940	Q 2XS	17.00	110
ARABIC II	601 × 65 × 48	15,801	Q 2XS	16.00	49-50
ARABIC III	590 × 70 × 39	16,785	Q 2XS	17.50	98
ATHENIC	500 × 63 × 45	12,234	Q 2XS	14.00	40-41
ATLANTIC	420 × 41 × 31	3,707	C 1XS	14.50	2

Name	Dimensions	Tonnage	Machinery	Speed	Page
BALTIC II	★ 729 × 76 × 37	23,875	Q 2XS	16.00	57-58
BARDIC	★ 465 × 58 × 29	8,010	T 2XS	14.00	94-95
BELGIC IV	670 × 78 × 45	24,547	T + LPT 3 XS	17.00	91
(Rebuilt)		27,132			
BRITANNIC I	455 × 45 × 34	5,004	C 1XS	15.00	6
BRITANNIC II	883 × 94 × 64	48,158	T + LPT 3XS	21.00	86-90
BRITANNIC III	684 × 82 × 53	26,943	D 2XS	18.00	113-11
BROUGHTON	172 × 28 × 18	580	Sail	N/A	119
CALGARIC	550 × 67 × 43	16,063	T + LPT 3XS	16.00	111
CANADA	500 × 58 × 31	8,800	T 2XS	15.00	47
CANOPIC	578 × 59 × 36	12,268	T 2XS	16.00	55
CEDRIC	★ 700 × 75 × 44	21,035	Q 2XS	16.00	44-46
CELTIC	437 × 41 × 31	3,867	C 1XS	14.00	5
CELTIC II	★ 700 × 75 × 44	20,904	Q 2XS	16.00	38-39
CERAMIC	655 × 69 × 44	18,495	T + LPT 3XS	15.50	83-84
CEVIC	★ 523 × 60 × 38	8,315	T 2XS	13.00	20
CORINTHIC	500 × 63 × 45	12,367	Q 2XS	14.00	42
CRETIC	582 × 60 × 38	13,518	T 2XS	15.00	52
CUFIC II	476 × 55 × 36	8,249	T 2XS	11.00	56
CYMRIC	585 × 64 × 38	13,096	Q 2XS	14.50	21
DORIC II	601 × 68 × 41	16,484	Tur 2XS	15.00	108
GALLIC I	150 × 28 × 10	461	C 2X Paddle	9.00	59
GALLIC II	★ 465 × 58 × 29	7,914	T 2XS	14.00	93
GEORGIC II	★ 712 × 82 × 53	27,759	D 2XS	18.00	116-118
GERMANIC	455 × 45 × 34	5,008	C 1XS	15.00	7-8
GOTHIC	491 × 53 × 33	7,755	T 2XS	14.00	18-19
HAVERFORD	531 × 59 × 27	11,635	T 2XS	14.00	97
HOMERIC	751 × 83 × 49	34,356	T 2XS	19.00	99-102
IONIC II	500 × 63 × 45	12,352	Q 2XS	14.00	43

Name	Dimensions	Tonnage	Machinery	Speed	Page
LAPLAND	606 × 70 × 37	17,540	Q 2XS	17.00	85
LAURENTIC I	550 × 67 × 41	14,892	T + LPT 3XS	17.00	62-63
LAURENTIC II	★600 × 75 × 41	18,724	T + LPT 3XS	17.00	112
MAGNETIC	170 × 32 × 15	619	T 2XS	13.75	17
MAJESTIC I	★581 × 58 × 39	9,965	T 2XS	19.00	14-15
MAJESTIC II	★955 × 100 × 58	56,551	Tur 4XS	23.50	103-106
MEDIC	★565 × 63 × 40	11,985	Q 2XS	13.50	23
MEGANTIC	550 × 67 × 41	14,878	Q 2XS	16.00	64-66
MERSEY	271 × 39 × 22	1,829	Sail	N/A	120
MOBILE	589 × 65 × 47	16,960	Q 2XS	16.00	96
NOMADIC I	461 × 49 × 31	1,273	T 2XS	12.00	16
OCEANIC I	420 × 41 × 31	3,707	C 1XS	14.00	1
OCEANIC II	★705 × 68 × 44	17,272	T 2XS	19.00	24-28
OLYMPIC	★882 × 92 × 59	45,234	T + LPT 3XS	21.00	68-73
(Rebuilt)		46,439			74
PERSIC	★565 × 63 × 40	11,973	T 2XS	13.50	29
PITTSBURGH	★601 × 68 × 41	16,332	T + LPT 3XS	15.00	107
REGINA	★601 × 68 × 41	16,313	T + LPT 3XS	15.00	109
REPUBLIC II	570 × 68 × 24	15,378	Q 2XS	16.00	53-54
ROMANIC	550 × 59 × 36	11,394	T 2XS	16.00	51
RUNIC II	★565 × 63 × 40	12,482	Q 2XS	13.50	30
SUEVIC	550 × 63 × 40	12,531	Q 2XS	13.50	31-37
TEUTONIC	★582 × 58 × 39	9,984	T 2XS	19.00	9-13
TITANIC	★883 × 92 × 59	46,328	T + LPT 3XS	21.00	76-82
VEDIC	460 × 58 × 37	9,302	Tur 2XS	14.00	92
VICTORIAN	512 × 59 × 35	8,825	T 1XS	13.00	48
ZEALANDIC	477 × 63 × 31	8,090	Q 2XS	13.00	75
ZEELAND	562 × 60 × 38	11,905	Q 2XS	15.00	67